American Short Stories

Exercises in Reading and Writing

Second Edition

Greg Costa

City College of San Francisco

Holt, Rinehart and Winston

A Division of Harcourt College Publishers

Philadelphia   San Diego   New York   Orlando   Austin   San Antonio
Toronto   Montreal   London   Sydney   Tokyo

Publisher	Phyllis Dobbins
Product Manager	Kenneth S. Kasee
Project Editor	Laurie Bondaz
Art Director	Garry Harman
Production Manager	Erin Gregg

Cover credit: "Days Gone By" by Paul Detlefsen. Art from the archives of Brown & Bigelow, Inc.

ISBN: 0-03-021334-7
Library of Congress Catalog Card Number: 99-067146

Address for Domestic Orders
Harcourt College Publishers, 6277 Sea Harbor Drive, Orlando, FL 32887-6777
800-782-4479

Address for International Orders
International Customer Service
Harcourt, Inc., 6277 Sea Harbor Drive, Orlando, FL 32887-6777
407-345-3800
(fax) 407-345-4060
(e-mail) hbintl@harcourtbrace.com

Address for Editorial Correspondence
Harcourt College Publishers, 301 Commerce Street, Suite 3700,
Fort Worth, TX 76102

Web Site Address
http://www.harcourtcollege.com

Printed in the United States of America

9 0 1 2 3 4 5 6 7 8 066 9 8 7 6 5 4 3 2 1

Holt, Rinehart and Winston

Harcourt College Publishers

**HOLT
RINEHART
WINSTON**

soon to become

A Harcourt Higher Learning Company

Soon you will find Holt, Rinehart & Winston's distinguished innovation, leadership, and support under a different name . . . a new brand that continues our unsurpassed quality, service, and commitment to education.

We are combining the strengths of our college imprints into one worldwide brand: Harcourt Our mission is to make learning accessible to anyone, anywhere, anytime—reinforcing our commitment to lifelong learning.

We'll soon be Harcourt College Publishers.
Ask for us by name.

One Company
**"Where Learning
Comes to Life."**

To Dr. Mo-Shuet Tam

Preface

I have adapted the nine stories in this book, these small treasures of American culture and history, so they can be shared with advanced learners of English—students still learning accuracy in reading and writing their second language.

The stories have been adapted to feature specific points of grammar in a meaningful context. Verb tenses, sentence patterns, and word forms are discussed and practiced in extensive exercises following each story. All the language in the grammar exercises comes from the stories, and each story uses the grammatical structures taught in the exercises.

While the purpose of the book is to increase a student's reading and writing skills, the stories and the American context in which they were written are so interesting that everyone should enjoy reading *American Short Stories*. Rich characters, clear plots and conflicts, and surprising resolutions make these stories entertaining to all readers, even those with limited English-language skills.

As students are talking, reading, and writing about the interesting American topics central to these stories, they will be practicing troublesome grammatical structures and learning to write accurately.

The second edition has been expanded and revised in several ways:

- Three new stories have been added. *American Short Stories* now contains enough fiction for most intermediate reading classes.
- New pre-reading sections introduce the author and the historical background of each story. Students are encouraged to make predictions and anticipate what they are going to read.
- Maps and graphs illustrate the history and development of the United States at the time each story was written. Exercises help students learn how to interpret the information.
- New reading exercises help students learn to analyze text for meaning, to break down fiction into more easily understandable parts.

Students who read *American Short Stories* will sharpen vocabulary skills and become better readers. They will learn to enjoy reading fiction as they are introduced to basic concepts of literary analysis and the rich heritage of American literature. They should gain a general understanding of how the United States began, grew, and developed into a modern industrial nation, and they should learn something of America's peoples and their struggles.

American Short Stories will prove to be both enjoyable and profitable to all who read it.

Greg Costa
San Francisco, California

Contents

The Bride Comes to Yellow Sky/Stephen Crane   98

An Occurrence at Owl Creek Bridge/Ambrose Bierce   125

Ten million eager immigrants entered the U. S. between 1860 and 1890

The Fat of the Land

Anzia Yezierska

THE AUTHOR

*Anzia Yezierska immigrated to the United States with
her Jewish family from Poland when she was just a small girl.
Poverty forced her to work in sweatshops during the day,
but hard work in night school earned her scholarships and
a teaching degree from Columbia University in 1904. She
married twice and had one daughter, but she did not find
her path in life until she met the philosopher and educator
John Dewey at Columbia in 1917. He encouraged her to write
about the immigrant community in which she grew up.
When "The Fat of the Land" won the O'Hare prize for best
short story of 1919, Anzia Yezierska finally found success. She
moved to Hollywood, where she became popular as a woman
who rose up from a poor background in the ghetto to become
a famous writer. Although she had some further success
during the 1920s, her career ended with the economic
depression of the 1930s. She died in obscurity in 1970,
well before her stories were rediscovered by a new
generation of American women.*

THE STORY

*"The Fat of the Land" is the story of a family divided by
two cultures. The main character, Hanneh Breineh, comes to
live in the United States as a married woman with six
children to raise. She keeps the culture of her old country,
Poland, but her children adopt American values and lifestyles
when they grow up.
In the first part of the story we see Hanneh Breineh in New
York City struggling to raise her children. The second part of
the story takes place years later, after the children have grown
up and become wealthy, successful Americans. But can they
make their old mother happy?
As we see in the story, the generation gap that often causes
problems between young and old can only be worse when the
older generation comes from a different world.*

I

Hanneh Breineh leaned out of her apartment into the airshaft and
knocked on her neighbor's window.

"Can you loan me your boiler for the clothes?" she called.

In 1878 The Statue of Liberty came to America from France, a gift for the 100th birthday of the United States. In this photo the head and shoulders of the giant statue wait to be moved to Liberty Island, in New York Harbor, where she stands today, greeting arriving immigrants like Anzia Yezierska, the author of "The Fat of the Land."

Mrs. Pelz lifted up the **sash**. "The boiler? What's the matter with yours again? Didn't you tell me you had it fixed already last week?" *[window]*

"Damn him, the robber, the way he fixed it! If you have no luck in this world, then it's better not to live. There I spent fifteen cents to stop one hole, and it runs out another. How I fought bargaining with him to get it down to fifteen cents! He wanted a quarter, the **swindler**. I curse him from my bitter heart for every penny he took from me for nothing!" *[crook, cheater]*

"You've got to watch all those swindlers, or they'll steal the whites out of your eyes," warned Mrs. Pelz. "You should have tried

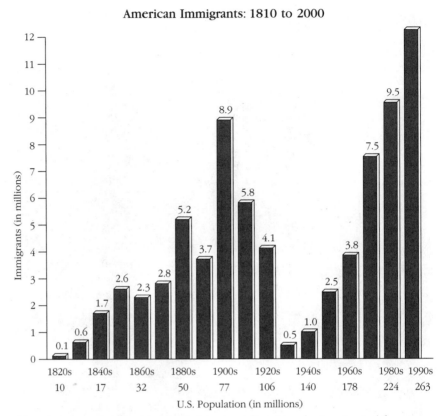

American Immigrants: 1810 to 2000

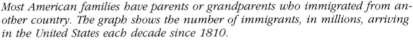

U.S. Population (in millions)

Most American families have parents or grandparents who immigrated from an-other country. The graph shows the number of immigrants, in millions, arriving in the United States each decade since 1810.

out your boiler before you paid him. Wait a minute until I empty out my dirty clothes in a pillow case, then I'll hand it to you."

Mrs. Pelz returned with the boiler and tried to hand it across to Hanneh Breineh, but it would not fit through the small window. "You've got to come in for the boiler yourself," said Mrs. Pelz.

"Wait until I tie my Sammy on to the high chair so he doesn't fall again. He's so wild that ropes won't hold him." Hanneh Breineh tied the child in the chair, stuck a **pacifier** in his mouth, and went in to her neighbor.

plastic nipple for sucking

As she took the boiler Mrs. Pelz said, "Do you know Mrs. Melker ordered fifty pounds of chicken for her daughter's wedding? And such fat chickens! My heart melted in me just looking at them."

Hanneh Breineh smacked her thin, dry lips, a hungry gleam in her sunken eyes. "Fifty pounds!" she gasped. "It isn't possible. How do you know?"

"I heard her with my own ears. I saw them with my own eyes. And she said she will chop up the chicken livers with onions and eggs for an appetizer, and then she will buy twenty-five pounds of fish, and cook it sweet and sour with raisins, and she said she will bake all her strudels in pure chicken fat."

"Some people work themselves up in the world," sighed Hanneh Breineh. "For them America is flowing with milk and honey. In the old country Mrs. Melker used to get **shriveled** up from hunger. She and her children used to live on potato peelings and crusts of dry bread, and in America she lives to eat chicken, and apple strudels soaked in fat."

shrunken and wrinkled

"The world is a wheel always turning," philosophized Mrs. Pelz. "Those who were high go down low, and those who have been low go up higher. Who will believe me here in America that in Poland I was a cook in a banker's house? I handled ducks and geese everyday. I used to bake coffee cake with cream so thick you could cut it with a knife."

"And do you think I was a nobody in Poland?" broke in Hanneh Breineh, tears filling her eyes as the memories of her past filled her mind. "But what is the use of talking? In America money is everything. Who cares who my father or grandfather was in Poland? Without money I am a living dead one. All I have time to think about is how to get the children something to eat for a penny cheaper."

Mrs. Pelz, filled with envy, nodded her head in agreement, "Mrs. Melker had it good from the day she came," she said, jealously. "Right away she sent all her children to the factory, and she began to cook meat for dinner everyday. She and her children have eggs and buttered rolls for breakfast each morning like millionaires."

There was a sudden fall and a baby's scream, and the boiler dropped from Hanneh Breineh's hands as she rushed into her kitchen, Mrs. Pelz following after her. They found the high chair turned over on top of the baby.

"Oh God! save me! Run for a doctor!" cried Hanneh Breineh, as she pulled the child from under the high chair. "He's dead! He's dead! My only child! My precious lamb!" she shrieked as she ran back and forth with the screaming infant.

Mrs. Pelz grabbed little Sammy from the mother's hands. "Calm down! Why are you running around like crazy, frightening the child? Let me see. Let me tend to him. He isn't dead yet." She ran to the sink to wash the child's face, and discovered a swelling lump on his forehead, but no serious injury.

making loving sounds

When he stopped crying, Hanneh Breineh took the child again in her arms, shaking and **cooing** over it and caressing it. "Ah-ah-ah, Sammy! Ah-ah-ah-ah, little lamb! Ah-ah-ah, little bird! Ah-ah-ah-ah, precious heart! I thought he had been killed!" Gasped Hanneh Breineh, turning to Mrs. Pelz. "Oh God" she sighed, "a mother's heart! Always in fear over her children. The minute anything happens to them all life goes out of me. I lose my head and I don't know where I am anymore. Why did I need yet the sixth one? Wasn't it enough to have five mouths to feed? If I didn't have this child on my neck, I could turn myself around and earn a few cents."

strongly criticized

"Shhh! Shhh!" **reproved** Mrs. Pelz. "Have pity on that child. Let it grow up already as long as it is here. See how frightened it looks hanging on to you!" Mrs. Pelz took the child in her arms and petted it. "Poor little lamb! What has it done that you should hate it so?"

painfully cried

Hanneh Breineh turned away from Mrs. Pelz in anger. "To whom can I open my heart?" she **moaned**. "Nobody has pity on me. You don't believe me, nobody will believe me until I fall down dead in the street. My life is so black! Some mothers have luck. A child gets run over by a car, some fall from a window, some burn themselves up with a match, some get choked with fever, but no death takes mine away."

warned gently

"My God! Stop cursing!" **admonished** Mrs. Pelz. "What do you want from the poor children? Is it their fault that their father makes small wages? Why do you take it all out on them? Mrs. Pelz put her arm around Hanneh Breineh. "Wait until your children get old enough to go to the shop and earn money," she consoled her. "Push yourself through these few years while they are still small, your sun will begin to shine, you will live on the fat of the land, when they begin to bring you their wages each week."

Hanneh Breineh refused to be comforted. "Until they are old enough to go to the shop and earn money they will eat us out of our home," she cried. "If only you knew the fights we have at each meal. Maybe I gave Abe a bigger piece of bread than Fanny. Maybe Fanny got a little more soup on her plate than Jake. Eating is
more expensive
dearer than diamonds. Potatoes went up a cent a pound, and milk is only for millionaires. And once a week, when I buy a little meat, the butcher weighs it for me like gold, with all the bones in it. When I lay the meat on a plate and divide it up, there is nothing to it but bones."

"Never mind. You will come out from all your troubles. Just as soon as your children get old enough to get their working papers the more children you got, the more money you will have."

"Why should I fool myself with false hope? Don't you know I have bad luck in this world? Do you think American children will give everything they earn to their mother?"

"I know what is the matter with you," said Mrs. Pelz. "You haven't eaten yet today. When the stomach is empty, the whole world looks black. Let me give you something good to taste. That will freshen you up." Mrs. Pelz went to the cupboard and brought a plate of *gefulte* fish that she had cooked for dinner and placed it on the table in front of Hanneh Breineh. "Give a taste to my fish," she said, taking one slice on a spoon, and handing it to Hanneh Breineh with a piece of bread. "I won't give it to you on a plate, because I just cleaned my kitchen, and I don't want to dirty my dishes."

"I'm not a stranger who you have to serve on a fancy plate!" cried Hanneh Breineh, **snatching** the fish in her **trembling** fingers. "Umm! Even the bones melt in my mouth!" she exclaimed, becoming more cheerful as she ate. "May this be good luck to us all!"

> **snatching** taking quickly
> **trembling** shaking

Mrs. Pelz was so **flattered** that she **ladled** up a spoonful of gravy. "There is a bit of onion and carrot in it," she said as she handed it to her neighbor.

> **flattered** happy to receive praise
> **ladled** served with a spoon

Hanneh Breineh sipped the gravy drop by drop, like a **connoisseur** sipping wine. "Ah-h-h! A taste of that gravy lifts me up to heaven." She relaxed as she leisurely ate the slice of onion and the carrot. But soon she remembered her other children.

> **connoisseur** expert on food and drink

"I'm forgetting everything," she exclaimed, jumping up. "It must be almost twelve, and my children will be right out of school and fall on me like a pack of wild wolves. I better quickly run to the market and see what I can get for them to eat."

Because she was late, the stale bread at the nearest bakery was sold out, and Hanneh had to go from shop to shop in search of the usual bargain, which took her nearly an hour to save two cents.

In the meantime the children returned from school, and, finding the door locked, climbed through the fire escape and entered the house through the window. Seeing nothing on the table, they rushed to the stove. Abe pulled a steaming potato out of the boiling pot, but dropped it to the floor as it **scalded** his fingers. Immediately the three others jumped on it.

> **scalded** burned with steam

"It was my potato," cried Abe, blowing on his burned fingers while with his foot he kicked the three who were struggling on the floor. A wild fight started, and the potato was smashed under Abe's foot amid shouts and screams.

Hanneh Breineh, on the stairs, heard the noise of her hungry children, and began to shout herself. "They are here already, the **savages**! They are here already to shorten my life! They heard you all over the hall, in all the houses around!"

uncivilized natives

The children, **disregarding** her words, grabbed at the groceries she was carrying, shouting "Mamma, I'm hungry! What do you have to eat?"

not listening

They tore the bag to get at the bread and herring and ate it with their fingers, all the time asking for more.

"You little pigs!" screamed Hanneh Breineh, **furious** with anger. "Calm down, all of you! Where do you think I can find the money to buy you any more? Here I had already cooked a pot of potatoes, bought a whole loaf of bread and two herrings, and you swallowed it down **in the wink of an eye**. It's impossible to fill your stomachs!"

violently angry

very quickly

Suddenly Hanneh Breineh became aware that Benny was missing. "Oh God!" she cried, wringing her hands in a new wave of despair, "where is Benny? Didn't he come home from school with you?"

She ran out into the hall, opened the window, and looked up and down the street, but Benny was nowhere in sight.

"Abe, Jake, Fanny, quick, find Benny!" ordered Hanneh Breineh, as she rushed back into the kitchen. But the children, **anxious** to play, **dodged** past her and hurried out and down the stairs.

not wanting to wait
quickly moved away

With the baby on her arm, Hanneh Breineh ran to the kindergarten. "Why are you keeping Benny here so long?" she shouted at the teacher as she ran into the classroom. "If you had a heart, you would send him home and not wait until I came for him."

The teacher turned calmly and answered the angry mother, "Benny Breineh was not present this morning."

"Not here!" **shrieked** Hanneh Breineh "I pushed him out the door myself this morning. The other children didn't want to take him, but I told them to wait. Oh my God! Where is my child?" She began pulling her hair and beating her breast as she ran into the street.

screamed loudly

Mrs. Pelz was just leaving the grocery store, when she heard the noise of an approaching crowd. A block away she recognized Hanneh Breineh, her hair a mess, her sweater unbuttoned, running toward her with her yelling baby in her arms, the crowd following.

"My friend," cried Hanneh Breineh, falling on Mrs. Pelz's neck, "I lost my Benny, the best child of all my children." Tears ran from her red, swollen eyes as she sobbed. "Benny! My heart, my life! Oh God! Oh God!"

Mrs. Pelz took the frightened baby out of the mother's arms. "Stop screaming! See how you are frightening your child."

"Where is my Benny? Maybe he has been killed by a car already. Maybe he **fainted** from hunger. He hasn't eaten anything all day long. Oh God please take pity on me! People, my child! Get me my child! I'll go crazy out of my head!"

"Stay still!" pleaded Mrs. Pelz.

"Don't talk to me!" cried Hanneh Breineh, wringing her hands. "You have all your children. I lost mine. Good luck only comes to other people. I haven't yet seen a good day in my life. My only joy, Benny, is lost from me forever."

The crowd followed Hanneh Breineh as she **wailed** through the streets, leaning on Mrs. Pelz. But just as she had returned to her house, and entered the kitchen with Mrs. Pelz, a policeman came in with the lost Benny.

"See, why did you **carry on** for nothing? Why did you shame yourself in the street?" said Mrs. Pelz.

The child's face was streaked with tears and he looked frightened and **forlorn**. Hanneh Breineh sprang toward him, slapping his cheeks and **boxing** his ears before her neighbor could rescue the child from her. "You bad boy!" cried the mother. "Don't I have enough worries already without having to go looking for you? You haven't given me a minute's peace since the day you were born."

"What a crazy mother!" criticized Mrs. Pelz, shielding the child from another beating, "What a mouth you have! With one breath she blesses him when he is lost, and with the other breath she curses him when he is found."

Hanneh Breineh dragged Benny over to the table and handed him a piece of bread. "Go eat!" commanded the mother. "Eat and choke yourself eating!"

II

"I wonder if she has forgotten who I am," thought Mrs. Pelz, as she walked by the brownstone house on Eighty-fourth Street where she had been told Hanneh Breineh now lived. After climbing the stairs, she was out of breath as she rang the bell with trembling fingers. "Even the outside smells rich! Look at those curtains! And expensive shades on all the windows like millionaires! Twenty years ago she used to eat from the pot with her fingers, and now she lives in a palace," she said to herself as the door opened. Inside, she saw

---

lost consciousness

cried

act in an unusual way

alone and unhappy
hitting, punching

apartments for the poor

her old friend of the **tenements** dressed in silk and diamonds like a being from another world.

"Mrs. Pelz, is it you?" cried Hanneh Breineh, overjoyed at the sight of her former neighbor. "Come right in. Since when have you been back in New York?"

spoke softly, unclearly

"We came last week," **mumbled** a surprised Mrs. Pelz, as she was led into a richly carpeted living room.

"Make yourself comfortable. Take off your coat," urged Hanneh Breineh.

But Mrs. Pelz only pulled her coat more tightly around her, thinking of her own poverty as she gazed at the luxurious wealth apparent in every corner of the room. "This coat covers up my

old, worn out

rags," she said, trying to hide her **shabby** dress.

"I'll tell you what, come right into the kitchen," suggested Hanneh Breineh. "The servant is away for this afternoon, and we can feel more comfortable there. I can breathe like a free person in my kitchen when the girl has her day off."

unclear state of mind

Mrs. Pelz looked around her in an excited **daze**. She had never seen anything so wonderful as this white tiled kitchen, with its shining porcelain sink and aluminum pots and pans that shone like silver.

"Where are you staying now?" asked Hanneh Breineh, as she pinned an apron over her silk dress.

"I moved back to Delancey Street, where we used to live," replied Mrs. Pelz, as she seated herself cautiously in a white enameled chair.

"Oh God! What grand times we had in that old house when we were neighbors!" sighed Hanneh Breineh, looking at her old

watery, almost crying

friend with **misty** eyes.

"Do you still think about Delancey Street? Don't you have more high class neighbors uptown here?"

"A good neighbor is not to be found everyday," sadly answered Hanneh Breineh. "Uptown here, where each family lives in his own house, nobody cares if the person next door is dying or going crazy from loneliness. It isn't anything like what we used to have in Delancey Street, when we could walk into one another's apartment without knocking, and borrow some salt or a pot to cook in."

Hanneh Breineh walked over to the counter. "We are going to have a bite right here on the kitchen table like on Delancey Street. So long as there is no maid to watch us we can eat what we please with our fingers."

"Ummh! how it waters my mouth with appetite, the smell of

the herring and onion!" laughed Mrs. Pelz, **sniffing** the welcome odors with greedy pleasure.

 Hanneh Breineh pulled a dish towel from the rack and placed it on the table. "So long as there is no servant around, we can use this for a tablecloth. It's dirty anyhow. It makes me so happy to see you!" she said as she poured them both a cup of tea. "I used to beg my daughter to write for me a letter to you, but these American children, they don't respect a mother's wishes."

 "What are you talking about!" cried Mrs. Pelz. "The whole world knows what success your children have had. Everybody is jealous of you. Tell me how your luck began."

 "You heard how my husband died on the job," replied Hanneh Breineh. "The five hundred dollars insurance money gave me the first lift in life, and I opened a little grocery store. Then my son Abe married a girl with a little money. That started him in business, and now he has the biggest shirt factory on West Twenty-ninth Street."

 "Yes, I heard your son had a factory." Mrs. Pelz hesitated with embarrassment. "I'll tell you the truth. What I came to ask you—I thought maybe you would beg your son Abe to give my husband a job."

 "Why not?" said Hanneh Breineh. "He has more than five hundred workers. I'll ask him if he can take care of Mr. Pelz."

 "Oh thank you so much, Hanneh Breineh! You'll save my life if you could only help my husband get work."

 "Of course my son will help him. All my children like to do good. My daughter Fanny is a dressmaker on Fifth Avenue, and she takes in the poorest girls in her shop and even pays them while they learn the trade." Hanneh Breineh's face lit up, and her chest filled with pride as she listed the successes of her children. "And my son Benny wrote a play on Broadway, and he gave away more than a hundred free tickets for the first night."

 "Benny? The one who used to get lost from home all the time? You always did love that child more than all the rest. And what is your baby Sammy doing?"

 "He's not a baby any longer. He goes to college and **quarterbacks** the football team. They can't get along without him. And my son Jake, I nearly forgot him. He owns apartment buildings. He started by buying a building on Delancey Street, and now he's collecting rent from some of the best buildings on Riverside Drive."

 "What did I tell you? In America children are like money in the bank," said Mrs. Pelz, as she **patted** her old friend's silk sleeve. "How lucky you are! You ought to kiss the sky and dance for joy

smelling

leads the team

touched affectionately

and happiness. It's so cold outside, and to heat our apartment is so expensive, and you have all the steam heat you want. I still owe for last month's rent, and you are rolling in money."

"Yes, I've got it good in some ways, but money isn't everything," sighed Hanneh Brcineh.

"You aren't satisfied yet?"

"But here I have no friends," complained Hanneh Breineh.

confused

"Friends?" asked a **puzzled** Mrs. Pelz. "What greater friend is there on earth than the dollar?"

"Oh Mrs. Pelz! If you could only look into my heart, you would see a sad, lonely old woman." Hanneh Breineh shook her head, and tears began to form in her eyes. "My children give me everything. When I was sick, they got me a nurse day and night. They bought me the best for my kitchen. If I asked for anything, they would give it to me, but I can't talk to them in their language. They want to make me into an American lady, and I'm different. When I was poor, I was free, and could yell and do what I like in my own house. Here, I have to watch everything I do and everything I say. Between living up to my high-class daughter and behaving well in front of the servants, I am like a prisoner in my own house." The doorbell rang, and Hanneh Breineh jumped in surprise.

"Oh no! It must be the maid back already." She exclaimed, as she tore off her apron. "Quickly, help me put the dishes in the sink. If she sees I have been eating on the kitchen table, she will look on me like the dirt under her feet."

Mrs. Pelz stood up quickly and got her coat. "I'd better leave quickly in these shabby clothes before your servant sees me."

"I'll speak to Abe about the job," said Hanneh Breineh, as she helped her friend out through the back door as the servant entered.

III

"**I'**m cooking fried potato *lotkes* especially for you, Benny," said Hanneh Breineh, as the children gathered around the table for the family dinner in honor of Benny's success with his new play. "Do you remember how you used to lick your fingers from them?"

poor ethnic neighborhood

"Oh Mother!" reproved Fanny. "Anyone hearing you would think we were still living in the **ghetto**."

repeated complaining
with love or kindness

Stop **nagging**, Sis, and leave Ma alone," said Benny, patting his mother's arm **affectionately**. "I never get a chance to eat at home. Let her feed me what she pleases."

"I heard that the president is coming to your play. Is that true?" asked Abe as he stuffed a napkin over his diamond-studded dress shirt.

"If you really want to know, he is coming tonight, and what's more, our box seats are next to the president's," returned Benny.

"Mama," interrupted Jake, "did you ever dream in Delancey Street that we should sit next to the president some day?"

"I always said that Benny had more brains than the rest of you," replied the mother.

After the laughter stopped, Jake continued, "I know you're getting famous, but are you making any money?"

"I'm getting ten percent **royalties** of the gross **receipts**," replied the youthful playwright.

"How much is that?" asked Hanneh Breineh.

"Enough to buy all the fish markets in Delancey Street," laughed Abe.

Her son's **teasing** cut like a knife in her heart. Hanneh Breineh felt her heart ache with the pain that she was shut out from their successes. "What worth is an old mother to American children? The president is coming tonight to the theater, and none of you asked me to go." Unable to fight back her rising tears, she ran into the kitchen and slammed the door.

"Say Sis," Benny called out sharply, "Haven't you told Mother that she was going with us tonight?"

"I'll take her some other time," **snapped** Fanny. "I don't care what you think! I can't appear with Mother in a box at the theater. Can I introduce her to Mrs. Van Suyden? Anyone will know we came from Delancey Street the minute we introduce her anywhere."

"But don't you have any feelings for Mother?" admonished Abe.

"I have tried harder than all of you to do my duty. I've lived with her." She turned angrily upon them. "I have to go with her everywhere while you buy her presents and holidays. God knows how hard I have tried to civilize her so I won't have to **blush** with shame when I take her anywhere. I have dressed her in the finest Parisian clothes, but whenever she opens her mouth, all that comes out is the voice of a poor old lady from Delancey Street."

The table was silenced by her anger, and they all turned unconsciously to Benny. "I guess we all have tried to do our best for Mother," he said, thoughtfully. "But wherever there is change, there is pain and heartbreak. The trouble with us is that we are children of the modern age and our Mother is from another world and another time, and—"

was heard loudly

The sound of crashing dishes came from the kitchen, and the voice of Hanneh Breineh **echoed** through the dining room as she screamed at the helpless servant.

"Oh my nerves! I can't stand it anymore! She'll quit for sure, and there will be no maid again for another week," cried Fanny.

"Oh, take it easy on the old lady," protested Abe. "Since she can't take it out on us anymore, what harm is it if she yells at the servants?"

"If you had to chase around to employment agencies, you wouldn't see anything funny about it."

small corner of a room used to cook food

"I have a good idea," said Jake, "I have a vacancy on Riverside Drive where there's only a small **kitchenette**, but cooking isn't necessary because the building has a dining service for the elderly who live there. This way she'll be taken care of, and she can't cause any problems."

IV

The new Riverside apartment to which Hanneh Breineh was removed by her **socially ambitious** children was, for the habitually

wanting to climb higher in society

active mother, no better than a lonely prison. When they took away her kitchen, Hanneh Breineh felt robbed of the last reason for her existence. Cooking and shopping and cleaning her pots and pans gave her an excuse for living and struggling and putting up with

deep sadness, despair

her children. The lonely idleness of Riverside Drive drove her to **depression**. She felt cut off from life, from everything warm and human. The cold indifference of the look in the eyes of the people around her were like slaps in the face.

But the worst part of the boring life on Riverside Drive was being forced to eat in the public dining room. No matter how hard she tried to learn polite table manners, she always found people staring at her, and her daughter criticizing her for eating with the

drinking very quickly spilling liquid which leaves a spot when dry

wrong fork, or **guzzling** the soup, or **staining** the tablecloth.

Finally one day Hanneh Breineh promised herself never to go down to the public dining room again, but to use the gas stove in the kitchenette to cook her own meals. To buy groceries, she took the train down to Delancey Street and her old familiar past. There Hanneh Breineh felt alive again as she pushed through the crowds of shoppers, filling her market basket with the best bargains she could find.

like a winner, very happy

Hanneh Breineh returned **triumphantly** with her purchases. The basket under her arm smelled of the old, homelike odors of herring and garlic, while the scaly tail of a four-pound fish stuck out from its newspaper wrapping. An engraved sign on the door of the apartment building stated that all merchandise must be delivered at the service entrance in the rear, but, without noticing it, Hanneh Breineh with her basket walked proudly through the marble paneled entrance hall and rang the bell for the elevator.

The uniformed door man stepped toward her with cold dignity. "Just a minute, madam. I'll call a boy to take your basket up for you," he said as he reached for the groceries.

Hanneh Breineh, glaring at him, jerked the basket back from his hands. "Mind your own business!" she shouted. "I'll take it up myself. Do you think you are a policeman to boss me in my own house?"

The doorman frowned, "It's against the rules, madam," he said stiffly.

"You should drop dead with your rules and fancy uniform. Is this America? Is this a free country? Can't I take up in my own house what I have bought with my own money?" yelled Hanneh Breineh, enjoying the chance to explode with the anger that she had held back for weeks since moving into the deadly dignified building on Riverside Drive.

Just then Hanneh Breineh saw Fanny come through the door. She rushed over to her, crying, "This bossy policeman won't let me take up my basket in the elevator."

The daughter, filled with shame and surprise, took the basket in her white gloved hand, gave it to the doorman, and ordered him to take it around to the delivery entrance.

Hanneh Breineh was so hurt by her daughter's defense of the doorman's rules that she turned away without saying another word and walked up the seven flights of stairs to her apartment in a **furious rage**.

> violent anger

Breathless from climbing the stairs, Hanneh Breineh entered the apartment just as Fanny came up in the elevator.

"Mother, you are ruining my life!" screamed Fanny. "Why do you think we got this apartment for you but to get rid of your fish smells and your fights with the servants? And here you come with a basket on your arm as if you just got off the boat from Poland yesterday! When will you ever stop **disgracing** us?"

> making someone publicly ashamed

"When I'm dead," answered the mother, "When the earth covers me up, then you will be free to go your American way. I'm not going to change myself into a fine lady of Riverside Drive for you. I hate you and all your swell friends. I won't let myself be bossed around by you or that doorman who you respect more than your own mother."

"So that's the thanks we get for all we have done for you?" cried Fanny.

"All you have done for me?" shouted Hanneh Breineh. "What have you done for me? You keep me like a dog on a chain. These clothes, this apartment, they are only things, and not things given with love."

"You want me to still love you?" raged the daughter. "You knocked every bit of love out of me when I was a kid. All the memories of childhood I have is your everlasting cursing and yelling that we were eating too much."

The doorbell rang and Hanneh Breineh answered it. "Your groceries ma'am," said the delivery boy.

Hanneh Breineh grabbed the basket from the surprised young man and threw it across the room in anger, sending the fish and vegetables flying over the Persian rugs and polished floor. Then, grabbing her hat and coat, she ran out of the apartment and down the stairs.

V

simple

Mr. and Mrs. Pelz sat eating their **modest** supper when the door opened, and Hanneh Breineh came into the room wearing her fur coat and feathered hat. "I've come to cry to you because I have nowhere else to go. My life is over!" she said.

"What is the matter with you, Hanneh Breineh?" cried Mrs. Pelz with worry and surprise.

"I am kicked out of my own house by the fancy uniformed policeman who bosses the elevator. Oh my God! what have I left in my life? The whole world is talking about my son's play, even the president came to see it, and I, his mother, have not seen it yet. My heart is dying in me," she went on crying. "I am starved for a piece of real food. In that swell restaurant there is nothing but napkins and forks and lettuce leaves. There are a dozen plates for every bite of solid food. It looks so fancy on the plate, but tastes like straw in my mouth. I'm starving, but I can't swallow their American food."

"Hanneh Breineh," said Mrs. Pelz, "you are sinning before God. Look at your fur coat. It alone would feed a whole family for a year. I never had a piece of fur **trimming** on a coat, and you are in fur from neck to feet. I never had a piece of feather on a hat, and your hat is all feathers."

material covering the
edges of a garment

"Why are you envying me?" protested Hanneh Breineh. "What have I got from all my fine furs and feathers when my children are strangers to me? All the fur coats in the world cannot warm up the loneliness inside my heart. All the feathers in the world cannot hide the bitter shame in my face when my children don't want to be seen with me.

"Why should my children be ashamed of me? Where did they get the stuff to work themselves up in the world? How did they get all their brains to rise above the people around them? Why don't the children of American born mothers write my Benny's plays? It is I, who never had a chance to live, who gave him the fire in his head. If I had had the chance to go to school and learn to read and write, what could I have been? It is I and my mother, and my mother's mother and my father and father's father who had such a black life in Poland. It is our choked thoughts and feelings that are coming out in my children and making them great in America, and yet they are ashamed of me!"

Mr. and Mrs. Pelz were speechless. Exhausted, Hanneh Breineh sat down and began to **weep** bitterly, her body shaking with **sobs**. "For what did I suffer and sacrifice for my children? For a bitter old age? I'm so lonely!"

cry
powerful cries of sadness

But Mr. and Mrs. Pelz saw the Hanneh Breineh of old, always unhappy, always complaining even now, surrounded by riches and plenty.

"Hanneh Breineh," said Mrs. Pelz, "the only trouble with you is that you have it too good. People will laugh at you because you're still complaining. If only I had your fur coat! If only I had your diamonds! I have nothing. You have everything. You are living on the fat of the land. You go right back home and thank God that you don't have to live my life."

"You have to let me stay here with you," **insisted** Hanneh Breineh. "I will not go back to my children except when they bury me. When they see my dead face, they will understand how they killed me."

commanded, said with force

Mrs. Pelz looked nervously at her husband. They barely had enough blankets for their one bed. How could they possibly make room for a visitor?

"I don't want to take your bed," said Hanneh Breineh. "I don't care if I have to sleep on the floor or on the chairs, but I need to stay here for the night."

Realizing that she was not going to leave, Mr. Pelz put some chairs together for himself, and Hanneh Breineh was invited to share the bed with Mrs. Pelz.

The mattress was full of **lumps**. Hanneh Breineh lay **cramped** and miserable, unable to stretch out her limbs. For years she had

solid bumps
not able to stretch out in a small space

been accustomed to firm mattresses and comfortable blankets, so she couldn't fall asleep. And as the lights were turned off, the mice came out and raced across the floor. The odors of the kitchen sink added to the night of horrors.

"Are you going back home?" asked Mrs. Pelz, as Hanneh Breineh put on her hat and coat the next morning.

"I don't know where I'm going," she replied, putting a bill into her old friend's hand as she walked out the door.

For hours Hanneh Breineh walked through the crowded ghetto streets. She realized that she no longer could **endure** the sordid ugliness of her past, and yet she could not go home to her children. She only felt that she must go on and on.

tolerate or accept

In the afternoon, a cold rain began. She was worn out from the sleepless night and hours of walking. With a pain in her heart she at last turned back and took the subway to Riverside Drive. She had fled from the **marble tomb** of the Riverside apartment to her old home in the ghetto, but now she knew that she could not live there again. She had outgrown her past. She could no longer do without the **material comforts** she had become used to over the years.

great stone cemetery monument

things purchased to make life easier

As Hanneh Breineh sadly approached the apartment house, she saw the uniformed doorman through the plate glass window. For a moment she stood in the **drizzling** rain, unable to enter, and yet knowing full well that she would have to go in eventually.

very light rain

Then suddenly Hanneh Breineh began to laugh. She realized that it was the first time she had laughed since her children had become rich. But it was the hard laugh of bitter sorrow. Tears streamed down her cheeks as she walked slowly up the granite steps. "The fat of the land!" muttered Hanneh Breineh, with a choking sob as the doorman politely swung open the door for her—"the fat of the land!"

Reading Comprehension

1. Hanneh Breineh immigrated to the United States from
   a. Poland.
   b. Russia.
   c. Germany.
2. Mrs. Pelz was her best friend because
   a. she came from the same country.
   b. she lived in the apartment next door.
   c. she had as many children as Hanneh Breineh.

3. Hanneh Breineh was the mother of
   a. five sons and one daughter.
   b. four sons and one daughter.
   c. four sons and two daughters.
4. When she was raising her children, Hanneh Breineh was unhappy because
   a. the family was poor.
   b. her husband died.
   c. she did not like living in America.
5. After her children grew up, Hanneh Breineh
   a. got divorced.
   b. lived a comfortable life.
   c. felt lonely and out of place.
6. Her daughter Fanny
   a. loved her mother.
   b. was ashamed of her mother.
   c. married a wealthy American.
7. Hanneh Breineh's children moved their mother to Riverside Drive because
   a. they wanted her to have every luxury possible.
   b. she was too old to live on Delancey Street.
   c. they wanted her to stop fighting with the maid.
8. She was not invited to her son Benny's play because
   a. Fanny did not want to be seen with her in public.
   b. her English was not good enough to understand it.
   c. it was sold out.
9. Hanneh Breineh was never happy in America because
   a. she didn't like the food and never learned English well.
   b. when she was poor she had too many children to raise, and when they grew up they did not take good care of her.
   c. when she was poor she had too many children to raise, and when they grew up, they did not respect her.

Vocabulary Check

Choose the sentence below that is closest in meaning to the model.

1. "Some people work themselves up in the world," sighed Hanneh Breineh. "For them America is flowing with milk and honey."
   a. Some people who start in America as poor immigrants easily make enough money to become wealthy.
   b. There is plenty to eat in the United States.
   c. Many immigrants work on farms when they come to America.

2. Hanneh Breineh turned away from Mrs. Pelz in anger. "To whom can I open my heart?" she moaned. "Nobody has pity on me."
   a. Hanneh Breineh has a weak heart and needs an operation.
   b. Hanneh Breineh feels that no one has sympathy for her and no one is willing to listen to her talk about her troubles.
   c. Hanneh Breineh doesn't love her husband anymore, but none of her friends understands her problem.

3. "You will live on the fat of the land, when they begin to bring you their wages each week."
   a. You will gain weight when you get old and your children have grown up.
   b. You can leave the city and live in the country when you retire.
   c. Your children will support you in luxury when they grow up and get good jobs.

4. "I bought a whole loaf of bread and two herrings, and you swallowed it down in the wink of an eye."
   a. You have eaten all the food I bought very quickly.
   b. As soon as I looked the other way, you ate all the food.
   c. Chew your food better before you swallow it.

5. Her son's teasing cut like a knife in her heart.
   a. Hanneh Breineh felt very sad when her son made a joke about her poor background.
   b. It made her proud to see her son cut the meat at dinner.
   c. She hated her son because he made fun of her.

6. "Oh, take it easy on the old lady. Since she can't take it out on us anymore, what harm is it if she yells at the servants?"
   a. Relax. Since we can't take her out to dinner, let her fight with the servants.
   b. Be kind to mother. Now that we are adults, she has no one to yell at but the servants.
   c. Mother is so old she will harm herself if she takes out the trash. Let the servants take it out.

7. Cooking and shopping and cleaning her pots and pans gave her an excuse for living and struggling and putting up with her children.
   a. taking care of her children.
   b. playing with her children.
   c. suffering without complaining about her children's demands.

8. "I don't know where I'm going," she replied, putting a bill into her old friend's hand as she walked out the door.
   a. giving her a bill to pay.
   b. giving her a $20 bill or larger.
   c. shaking her hand in friendship.

Story Summary

"The Fat of the Land" is a story told in five parts. For a clear understanding of the plot, write a sentence describing what happens in each of the five parts.

1. _____

_____

2. _____

_____

3. _____

_____

4. _____

_____

5. _____

_____

Analyzing the Text

Hanneh Breineh: Differing points of view

Who is Hanneh Breineh? Is she a good mother who sacrificed her life to raise her children, or is she selfish and ungrateful? Different characters in the story have different opinions of her. Reread parts III and IV to see what her children say about her, then parts II and V to see what her friend Mrs. Pelz thinks. What does Hannah herself believe? Do different readers also have different ideas about her character? Discuss these opinions and find facts in the story to support your conclusions.

In the spaces provided below, write what you think each of the following would say about Hanneh Breineh.

Her children think she _____

_____

_____

Mrs. Pelz thinks she _____

_____

_____

Hanneh Breineh thinks she _____

_____

_____

You, the reader, think she _____

_____

_____

Interpreting Graphs

Look at the graph on page 4 showing U.S. immigration from 1810 to 2000. It shows that the numbers of people immigrating has changed greatly over time. Study the graph to find the information you need to answer the following questions:

1. When were the decades of greatest immigration?
2. How many people immigrated to the United States between 1900 and 1920?
3. How many people immigrated between 1970 and 1999?
4. How many people immigrated between 1930 and 1950?
5. What are some historical reasons for these changing numbers?
6. Immigration numbers for the 1900s and 1980s are almost the same, but the country grew greatly in the twentieth century. Compare the total population for both periods.

Grammar and Sentence Writing

Past Perfect Tense and Simple Past Tense

The past perfect tense can be used to describe an action that occurred before another, related past action.

Before she <u>moved</u> uptown, Hanneh Breineh <u>had lived</u> in a poor neighborhood.

"Moved" is written in the past tense, but "had lived" is in the past perfect form because this action happened first, or before "moving."

To form the past perfect tense, use the simple past form of *have* followed by the past participle of the main verb. Note that the past participle is not always the same as the simple past form of the same verb:

We <u>ate</u> potato *lotkes* last night, but we <u>had never eaten</u> Polish food before.

Sentence Writing

In the sentences below, verbs in the past perfect tense (*had cooked*) are actions that occurred before the action described in the past tense (*brought a plate*). Rewrite the sentences as in the model below, using only the simple past tense for all verbs.

MODEL:

Mrs. Pelz went to the cupboard and brought a plate of *gefulte* fish that she had cooked for dinner and placed it on the table in front of Hanneh Breineh.

First Mrs. Pelz *cooked a plate of gefulte fish for dinner*

and then *she brought and placed it on the table in front of Hanneh Breineh.*

1. Here I had already cooked a pot of potatoes, bought a whole loaf of bread and two herrings, and you swallowed it down in the wink of an eye.

First I _____

and then you _____

2. But just as she had returned to her house, and entered the kitchen with Mrs. Pelz, a policeman came in with the lost Benny.

First she _____

and then a policeman _____

3. Mrs. Pelz walked to the brownstone house on Eighty-fourth Street where she had been told Hanneh Breineh now lived.

First Mrs. Pelz _____

and then she _____

4. Hanneh Breineh had always been complaining about her life when she was poor, and now that she was rich she still was complaining.

First Hanneh Breineh _____

and then when she was rich _____

5. For years she had been accustomed to firm mattresses and comfortable blankets, so she couldn't fall asleep.

First she _____

and then she _____

6. She had fled from the marble tomb of the Riverside apartment to her old home in the ghetto, but now she realized that she could not live there again.

First she _____

and then she _____

7. She could no longer do without the material comforts she had become used to over the years.

First she _____

and then she _____

8. She had not laughed since she became rich.

She used to _____

before she _____

9. She realized she had outgrown her past.

First she _____

and then she _____

Sentence Writing

Combine each pair of the sentences below to form a complex sentence, one clause with the verb in the past perfect tense (_had cooked_) and the other clause with the action described in the past tense (_brought a plate_). See page 22 to review the difference between past perfect and simple past tenses.

MODEL:
Mrs. Pelz placed a plate of _gefulte_ fish on the table in front of Hanneh Breineh.
Mrs. Pelz cooked it for dinner. (that)

**Mrs. Pelz placed a plate of gefulte fish that she had cooked for dinner on the table in front of Hanneh Breineh.**

MODEL:
Benny was a difficult child to raise.
He became famous when he grew up. (who)

**Benny, who had been a difficult child to raise, became famous when he grew up.**

1. Hanneh Breineh paid a workman to fix her boiler.
   It was still broken. (but)

   _____

   _____

2. Hanneh Breineh tied Sammy to his high chair.
   He tipped the chair over. (but)

   _____

   _____

3. Hanneh Breineh's stomach was empty.
   She did not eat anything all day. (because)

   _____

   _____

4. Hanneh Breineh's life became much easier.
   Her children grew up and went to work. (after)

   _____

   _____

5. She was crying for her lost son Benny.
   A policeman brought him home. (before)

   _____

   _____

6. Mrs. Pelz found out that Hanneh Breineh was living on Eighty-fourth
   Street.
   She went to visit her. (before)

   _____

   _____

7. Fanny did not tell her brothers.
   She did not invite their mother to the play. (that)

   _____

   _____

8. Fanny hated her mother.
   Her mother always yelled at her when she was a child. (because)

   _____

   _____

Word Forms

Choose the correct word to complete each sentence below.

Poor   Poverty   Poorest

1. Mrs. Pelz was thinking of her own _____ as she gazed at the luxurious wealth apparent in every corner of the room.

2. My daughter Fanny takes in the _____ girls in her shop and even pays them while they learn the trade.

3. When I was _____, I was free, and could yell and do what I liked in my own house.

Immigrant   Immigration   Immigrate

1. Hanneh Breineh was a poor _____ from Poland.

2. People from many countries _____ to the United States each year.

3. _____ to the United States changed Hanneh Breineh's life.

Hunger   Hungry   Hungrily

1. Hanneh Breineh, on the stairs, heard the noise of her _____ children.

2. "Where is my Benny? Maybe he has been killed by a car already. Maybe he fainted from _____!"

3. Hanneh Breineh _____ ate the fish her neighbor placed on the table.

Anger   Angry   Angrily

1. "Eat and choke yourself eating!" Hanneh Breineh _____ shouted at Benny.

2. The teacher turned calmly and answered the _____ mother, "Benny Breineh was not present this morning."

3. Hanneh Breineh exploded with the _____ that she had held back for weeks since moving into the building on Riverside Drive.

Jealousy   Jealous   Jealously

1. "Mrs. Melker had it good from the day she came," she said, _____ "Right away she sent all her children to the factory."

2. "The whole world knows what success your children have had. Everybody is _____ of you."

3. When Mrs. Pelz saw her old friend's beautiful home, she had to swallow her feelings of _____ .

Developing Ideas

Paragraph Writing

The Rich and the Poor in the City   1. Hanneh Breineh experienced both sides of life in New York. As a new immigrant, she lived in the slums of Delancey Street. Later in life, her children's success enabled her to move to the luxury of Riverside Drive. Her friend Mrs. Pelz, who never had the chance to move up in the world, cannot understand why Hanneh is not happy with her newfound life of ease. Shouldn't the woman be grateful for her good fortune? Is it realistic to think that many who find themselves in Hanneh Breineh's position would be equally unhappy? What is the connection between wealth and happiness?

Should We Devote Our Lives to Our Children?   2. Many immigrants endure difficult lives when they first come to the United States, but the dream of a better future for their children keeps them going. But the children of immigrants grow up differently than their parents expect because they are in a different country, with new values and new ideas. Misunderstandings like those between Hanneh and her children are common in such families. Is it worth the struggle to sacrifice for your children? Do immigrants have a harder time raising their children than native-born Americans?

Has Life Changed Since the Days of "Fat of the Land"?   3. As the graph at the beginning of the story shows, Anzia Yezierska grew up in a time when a great wave of immigrants was adapting to life in America. This wave of immigration can be compared to today's great migration of newcomers to the United States. Similarly, large cities like New York are home today to many new immigrants. How are conditions different today? How are they the same?

Topics for Discussion

1. Immigrant families: conflicts between parents and children

What are common sources of conflict between immigrants and their children? Do parents have realistic expectations for their children? Do most immigrant families have the kind of problems we read about in "The Fat of the Land"?

2. Was Hanneh Breineh a good mother?

Struggling with little money to raise six children, Hanneh Breineh often lost her temper and said terrible things to them. Once in the story, she even told Mrs. Pelz that she wished that her children would die in some kind of accident. Did she mean what she said? Is it surprising that she talked the way she did? Did she raise them well, or could she have done a better job? Does she really love her children?

3. Do children owe their parents love and respect?

Near the end of the story, Fanny loses her temper and tells her mother "You knocked every bit of love out of me when I was a kid." Instead of protecting her mother from the snobbish doorman, she takes his side in the argument about her smelly fish. Should Fanny treat her mother like this? It is clear that Hanneh Breineh was not a perfect mother to her small children, but do they have the right to criticize her after they have grown up? Can parents be held responsible for their past mistakes by their grown children?

For Further Discussion: The Character of Hanneh Breineh

A character is a person created in a work of fiction: a short story, novel, play, poem, or movie. Characters come alive through their actions and speech, and sometimes by revealing their thoughts. Fictitious characters—like Santa Claus—can be bigger than life. Hanneh Breineh is a good example of a complicated, well-rounded character with an interesting personality. She is not easy to forget. After reading "The Fat of the Land" many readers are not sure how to judge her. We respect her as a mother, but we see that she says and does things that most of us would criticize. Anzia Yezierska has created someone very much like a real person: surprising, unusual, and with both good and bad characteristics. Her life story is neither an unqualified success nor a total disaster, much like real people in the real world.

- Make a list of remarkable things Hanneh Breineh does and says that make her an unforgettable character. Include the outrageous things she says and the surprising things she does when she is both poor and rich.
- Compare Hanneh Breineh with other memorable characters you have come to know through literature, movies, or TV. To be remembered, each great character has to stand out from the rest, or be *unique*, but can you think of ways they are all similar?

South of
The Slot

JACK LONDON

THE AUTHOR

Born in San Francisco in 1876, Jack London grew up in nearby working-class Oakland to become one of America's most popular writers. His family was so poor that he was forced to begin working when only ten years old. After leaving Oakland, London rode freight trains with hobos across the United States, sailed as a common seaman to Asia, and served time in jail for vagrancy. In 1896, when gold was discovered in the Yukon, London caught gold fever and followed thousands of other unemployed young men to Alaska. He didn't find any gold, but from the experience he wrote Call of the Wild, *a novel that ensured his success as a writer. After reading the works of Karl Marx, London (whose photograph accompanies this selection) became a socialist. In "South of The Slot" his sympathies with the workers are obvious.*

THE STORY

"South of The Slot" is a story of inner conflict within one character—Freddie Drummond, a sociology professor at the University of California at Berkeley. This battle symbolized a much larger struggle: the fight between newly formed labor unions and the rich who ruled San Francisco society at the turn of the twentieth century. At that time, laborers worked long hours in poor conditions for small wages.
The Berkeley professor has a good position in society, but his work takes him into a new world of workers and poverty unknown to others of his social class. Surprisingly, Professor Drummond finds life south of The Slot more attractive than the lifestyles of the wealthy and well-educated people he leaves behind him.
Even in today's society and improved working conditions, could anyone argue that ordinary laborers have better lives than the rich? Do the poor have anything that the wealthy do not have? Would Jack London still prefer to live among the poor if he were alive today?

In the old days of San Francisco, before the Great Earthquake of 1906, the city was divided into two sections by the slot. The Slot was an iron crack in the center of Market Street through which ran

Market Street, San Francisco, was crowded with streetcars in the days of Jack London. Today, underground tracks link the city's main artery with Berkeley and the University of California, where Freddie Drummond, the main character of "South of the Slot," taught sociology.

the moving cable which pulled cable cars on the city's main street. Actually, there were two slots and two cables so that the cable cars could be pulled both uphill and downhill, but San Francisco simply called them, and all of Market Street, The Slot.

North of the Slot were theaters, hotels, and expensive stores. Banks and respectable businesses had their offices here, and the houses on the hills north of Market Street were large and **luxurious**. South of The Slot were factories, **slums**, laundries, warehouses, railroad yards, and the homes of the working class. So The Slot was more than a busy street; it separated the rich from the poor.

very comfortable

areas of crowded, rundown housing

The Slot **symbolized** the class distinction of society. Those who lived north of Market rarely crossed to go south, and those who lived south of The Slot rarely went north across Market, except when their work took them into the kitchens, cellars, and department stores of the **wealthy**.

But there was one man who crossed this symbolic border as easily as he crossed any street. This man was Professor Freddie Drummond. He lived in both worlds, working class and upper class, and in both worlds he lived very well. Freddie Drummond was a professor of **sociology** at the University of California, across the bay in Berkeley. He first crossed over The Slot while doing sociological **research**. He lived and worked south of Market for six months while he was writing *The Unskilled Laborer,* about the workers in the factories and **mills** of America. To gather information about the subjects of his book, he pretended to be a common laborer, working in various factories in the working-class district.

When he first crossed Market Street wearing a workingman's cap and carrying a lunchbox, Freddie Drummond had a hard time making friends with the other laborers. He was not used to their ways, and they were not used to his. They were **suspicious** because his hands were too soft and he was too polite. To explain his upper-class speech and **manners**, he pretended to be a man who once had been wealthy, but had lost his fortune through bad luck.

Gradually, Drummond was accepted by his workmates. Living south of Market, he learned many things, and reported them all in *The Unskilled Laborer*. In those six months he worked at different jobs and learned how to do a very good **imitation** of a genuine worker. He was a natural **linguist**, and he kept a notebook of the workers' **slang** while he was working with them. Soon he could talk in a friendly manner with the workers, and collect information for his study of working-class **psychology**. He conquered his fear of the laboring classes. If he wanted to, he could cross The Slot at any time and easily fit into life south of Market.

His first book was so successful that he soon crossed south of The Slot again to write a second book, in which he claimed "to really know the working people by working beside them, eating their food, sleeping in their beds, thinking their thoughts, and feeling their feelings."

When his second book was published, Freddie Drummond became a **celebrity**. Bankers and businessmen everywhere agreed

Glossary:
- stood for, was an example of
- rich
- the study of how human society is formed and how it functions / scientific investigation
- buildings where industrial materials are made or processed
- distrustful, fearful that something is not what it seems to be
- customary ways of acting
- bit by bit, as time went by
- pretense that one is someone else
- student of languages
- informal language
- the workings of the mind of a person or class of persons
- famous person

with his works, which stated that the ordinary working man "suffered from a serious lack of ambition . . . could be expected to do as little productive work as possible . . . and, if given the chance, would steal anything he could." In general, the professor wrote that the working man was a lazy, ignorant **brute** who, when given holidays from work and money to spend, would only get drunk and into fights and other terrible trouble.

> beast, animal without sense

Of course, these ideas about the working class were very popular at all the **fashionable** dinner parties on Nob Hill, so Freddie Drummond was soon a popular member of high society. But the professor, who had always been shy, was not comfortable at parties. While he was a student in college, he never **socialized** and had little time for friends. His schoolmates thought he was **antisocial**, but his constant studying had earned him a Ph.D. at the age of twenty-seven. He was a very quiet man, and had never had many friends. He had no **vices**, nor had he ever discovered any **temptations**. He hated tobacco, and beer made him sick. He never drank anything stronger than a light wine at dinner.

> stylish, up-to-date

> mingled with other people / unfriendly

> bad habits / encouragements to do wrong

On the other hand, south of Market, where he called himself "Big" Bill Totts, he was known to drink and smoke, and to **cuss** and fight. Everybody liked Bill, and more than one working girl was in love with him. At first, when he was afraid his working-class **companions** would discover his true **identity**, his wild behavior had been only to show them that he was a typical laborer. But as time went on, he began to enjoy drinking in beer halls, dancing with the girls, and eating in **greasy spoons**. In fact, he found himself **regretting** the times he had to return to his classroom as Professor Drummond. When he was in Berkeley, he often dreamed of his next adventure south of The Slot. Big Bill Totts could do many things that Freddie Drummond would never have been permitted to do.

> curse: use profane language, swear

> friends / nature, character

> common lunch counters, cafés / feeling sorry about

It was as if Freddie Drummond and Bill Totts were two totally different people. While he was on the job, Bill Totts worked as slowly as possible, **chatting** with the girls until a **foreman** caught him and sent him back to work. On the other hand, Freddie Drummond **condemned** lazy workers as un-American, unproductive, and unpatriotic. Freddie Drummond did not enjoy dancing, but Big Bill Totts never missed a night at the Flamingo Dance Hall, where he won first prize as best dancer at the Butchers' and Meatworkers' Annual Grand Masked Ball. Bill Totts liked the girls and the girls liked him, but Freddie Drummond had few female friends and felt

> casually talking / floor boss

> expressed strong disapproval of

uncomfortable when talking with the young women in his university classes.

When Freddie Drummond changed his clothes to become a working man, he changed his manners too. Professor Drummond was quiet, polite, and very **formal**. But when he wore Bill Totts' clothes he acted differently. He laughed often and **heartily**, and his talk was filled with swear words. Also, Bill Totts enjoyed staying out late at night, drinking beer, and having fun with other working men. He was at every Sunday picnic, walking with a girl on each arm, laughing and joking.

Bill Totts felt so comfortable with working-class life that when he was working on the **docks**, and the Longshoremen's Union called a strike, he was there with the strikers on the **picket line**. And when the **scabs** tried to cross the line to take Bill's job, he joined in the fight. The situation was now very strange. Bill Totts was **punching** scabs and policemen on the docks of San Francisco one day, and the next day, Professor Drummond was **criticizing** the strikers from his classroom in Berkeley.

Soon after this Freddie Drummond realized that he could have serious problems with Bill Totts—the man he had created. This was because while collecting information for a third book, *Women and Work*, Bill Totts fell in love.

Her name was Mary Condon, President of the International Glove Workers Union Number 974. He had first seen her at a union meeting when she was giving a **rousing** speech. He had seen her through Bill Totts' eyes, and that young man **had been impressed with** her dark-haired beauty and her powerful voice, which filled with passion when speaking of the suffering of the working class.

If Freddie Drummond had met her in Berkeley, he would not have been attracted to such a wild woman, but Bill Totts liked her from the moment he first saw her. He found out who she was and waited for a chance to meet her.

Within a few weeks he ran into her. While working as a delivery truck driver, Totts was called to remove a **trunk** from a **boarding house** on Mission Street. The trunk belonged to a sick member of the Glovemakers Union who was now in the hospital. Mary Condon had stopped by to help pay the sick union member's rent, when she saw Big Bill **struggling** with the heavy load.

"Hey there! Do you belong to the **Teamsters** Union?" she asked.

Margin glossary:

socially correct, observant of rules and customs / with emotion, from the heart

place for loading and unloading cargo from ships / line of striking workers stationed outside their place of work to try to stop other workers or customers from entering / persons who take the jobs of striking workers / hitting with his fists / speaking against

exciting
had admired, had been struck by

large, suitcase-like container / place where rooms and meals may be obtained for payment

working hard

persons who drive trucks for hauling

"Aw, what's it to you?" he answered. "Can't you see this thing is heavy? Run along now, so I can do my work."

The next thing he knew, he was thrown against the wall, his back **straining** under the weight of his load. He started to swear, but then found himself staring into the flashing, angry eyes of Mary Condon.

undergoing pressure or stress

"Of course I belong to the union," he said. "I was only kidding you."

"If you were in the union, you would have a union card. Where's your union card?" she demanded.

"It's in my pocket, but I can't get it now. This trunk is too damn heavy. If you came down to the truck, I'd show it to you."

"Put that trunk down!" she ordered.

"What for? I've got a card! I'm telling you the truth!"

"Put it down, that's all. No scab's going to handle that trunk. You ought to be ashamed of yourself, you big **coward**. Why don't you join the union and be a man?" Mary Condon was in a rage.

person who lacks courage

"Hold on now, that's too much!" Bill dropped the trunk to the floor with a bang, straightened up, and pulled out his card from his inside coat pocket. "I told you I was only kiddin'. There, look at that."

It was indeed a union card.

"All right, take it along." Mary Condon said. "And next time don't kid."

She relaxed as she noticed how easily Big Bill lifted the trunk back up onto his shoulders. But Bill, who was too busy with his heavy load, didn't see her watching him.

The next time he saw Mary Condon was during the Laundry Strike. Professor Drummond had sent Bill Totts to join the union and **investigate**. But the professor did not know that Mary Condon was there to organize the strike. When Totts arrived at the scene and saw Mary, he forgot all about Freddie Drummond.

examine deeply

Mary was at the gate of the factory, arguing with a big fat man who was standing in the entrance. He, the plant **superintendent**, would not let Mary enter to talk to the workers. As Mary tried to squeeze past him, she was pushed back, almost into the arms of Bill.

person in charge, head boss

She looked up, and without showing surprise, said, "Here you, Mr. Totts, give me a hand. If I were as big as you, I wouldn't have any trouble pushing past this fat boss! Help me get in."

Bill was surprised that she had remembered his name from his union card. He easily pushed the boss out of the way, and Mary went inside. Within half an hour all the workers had walked out on strike. During the entire strike that followed, while Mary talked to the workers and attended meetings, Bill accompanied her as a person bodyguard and messenger. Only when the strike was over did he return to the university to be Freddie Drummond, who couldn't understand why Bill Totts was so **attracted to** such a woman.

Freddie Drummond was entirely safe, but Bill had fallen in love. There was no **denying** it, and this frightened Drummond into making some changes. Well, he had done his work, and his adventures would stop. There was no need for him to cross The Slot again. Since his latest book was almost finished, he had no need to **pose** as a working man any longer.

Another change he decided upon was to form closer **relationships** with his own social class. If he had a woman of his own kind, he wouldn't think about Mary Condon so much. It was time that he was married, and if Freddie Drummond didn't get married, Bill Totts surely would. Freddie Drummond **shuddered** at the thought of being married to a wild-eyed labor organizer like Mary Condon. And so, Freddie began seeing Catherine Van Vorst. She was a college woman herself, and her father, a very wealthy man, was the head of the Philosophy Department. When Freddie Drummond announced the **engagement**, everyone thought it would be a wise marriage. **Aristocratic** Catherine, though coldly beautiful, was **reserved** and conservative—a good partner for Professor Drummond.

But Freddie could not forget the happy, irresponsible life he had enjoyed south of The Slot. He decided he needed one last wild adventure south of Market. So Freddie Drummond went down for the last time as Bill Totts, and unfortunately, **encountered** Mary Condon. Bill Totts lost control of himself. Not only did he run into her at the Central Labor Council, but he stopped at a coffee shop with her on the way home, and treated her to dinner. And before they parted at her door, his arms went around her, and he kissed her on the lips and kissed her **repeatedly**. And her last words in his ear, words spoken softly with a cry in her throat, were "Bill, dear, dear, Bill."

When he got back to Berkeley, Professor Drummond was **horrified**. He saw the danger before him. Since he was not by nature a **polygamist**, he was frightened of the possibilities. He promised himself that he would never go south of The Slot as Big Bill Totts again.

So for several months Professor Drummond stayed north of

Margin glossary:

drawn toward, interested in

saying it was not true

pretend to be what one is not / friendships

shook with fear and disgust

formal plan to get married / of the highest social class / cautious in words and actions

ran into unexpectedly

again and again

greatly frightened

man who has more than one wife at the same time

Market, spending his time with Catherine Van Vorst, while the laborers and their bosses fought many **battles** south of The Slot. Drummond was **tempted** to go south of The Slot during the Street Car Strike, but he **resisted** and stayed in Berkeley. Even now, as the Great Meat Strike was in its third week, Freddie Drummond stayed home at the university. He didn't know what Bill Totts would do if he crossed south of Market.

But now, with the wedding only two weeks away, he and Catherine had to go to San Francisco one afternoon to choose the flowers for the **ceremony**. Catherine was driving him down Market so they could turn and go up Geary Street to the **florist's** shop. Unfortunately, they did not know what was coming toward them down Geary.

Although the professor knew that the Meat Strike was still going on and that it was a very **bitter** fight, at that moment he wasn't thinking about labor problems. He was sitting beside Catherine, listening to her talk about the flowers she had chosen for the church. But coming down Geary Street were six meat trucks, driven by scab drivers. A policeman sat beside each driver, and alongside marched **troops** of police. An angry, howling mob of strikers and their **sympathizers** followed behind this army of police.

If the meat companies were able to deliver meat to the big hotels, they could beat the strike. The Saint Francis Hotel had already been supplied, although the hotel **suffered** many broken windows and the strikers many broken heads. Now the fight moved on to the Palace Hotel.

Meanwhile, Drummond was paying attention to Catherine as she continued to talk about their wedding. Suddenly their car stopped. Drummond looked away from Catherine to see that they were in the middle of a large traffic jam of delivery trucks, policemen, strikers, and general city traffic.

Market Street was a mess: The police surrounded the meat trucks, the mob was behind them, and directly in front of Catherine's car, a large coal truck was stopped, blocking all lanes of traffic.

If the coal truck moved, the meat truck and the police could proceed. But the driver of the truck was a union man, and he was in no hurry to clear the street. Suddenly other workers ran into the **intersection**. But there was no way Catherine could move her car.

"We're in for it," Drummond said coolly to Catherine.

"Yes," she said, equally cool. "What **savages** they are."

When Freddie saw how calmly Catherine sat there watching

---

conflicts, violent fights

lured, attracted

struggled against

formal or solemn rite

flower seller's

harsh, intensely hostile

organized groups (of police or soldiers) / supporters

received wounds or injuries

place where two streets come together

uncivilized people

the **riot**, his heart filled with love. If she had screamed and held him tightly, he would have understood her fear. But instead, she sat quietly, with **dignity**, above the excitement.

Meanwhile, the driver of the coal truck had refused to move. The police were battling the crowd to get to the truck. If they got the driver out, they could move the truck themselves. But the crowd was **stubborn**. The police swung their sticks, and the strikers fought back.

Just as the police were ready to open the door of the meat truck and pull out the driver, a young woman jumped up onto the coal piled high in the back of the truck, and began throwing huge **lumps** at the police nearest the driver's door. They had to move back because of her **furious** attack. Now other troops tried to climb into the truck from the rear, but the wild woman turned just in time to **hurl** a huge piece of black coal at the cops, and they fell back to the pavement. The crowd yelled in support of this woman who was fighting an army of police.

And Freddie Drummond yelled too, because when the young woman turned to throw coal at the police climbing up on the truck, he suddenly saw that she was Mary Condon!

"Can you imagine, Freddie! Even their women have no respect for the law," cried Catherine, amazed that one of **the gentler sex** would battle so fearlessly with the police.

But Freddie didn't answer, because Freddie wasn't listening. The moment he recognized Mary, he became Big Bill Totts. His sweetheart was in danger. This was the same woman he had protected during the Laundry Strike, the same one who had kissed him so passionately not long before. Even if he wanted to stay safely in the auto, he couldn't control himself.

Although Freddie Drummond had been **transformed** into Big Bill Totts when he saw Mary Condon battling the police, unfortunately he was still sitting next to Catherine Van Vorst. She, too, saw the strange battle in front of her, and then she saw an even stranger sight.

She saw the man beside her leap from the car with a wild yell, run through the crowd, and jump atop the coal truck. A police officer who was ready to grab Mary from behind stopped to see what this well-dressed but excited gentleman wanted to say to him, and was surprised with a punch to the jaw that knocked him to the ground. The crowd roared encouragement, while Mary and Bill kept the police away from the wagon with a steady **barrage** of coal.

destructive violence by a mob
calm and noble manner
determined not to give up
large pieces
wildly angry
throw hard
term sometimes used to mean women in general
changed
attack of bombs or missiles

Catherine Van Vorst watched with **amazement** as her **fiancé** and this wild, black-haired woman fought the cops while the mob behind broke through the police lines, overturned the meat trucks, and sent the scabs and the police running in every direction.

great surprise / man engaged to be married

"Now's our chance, Bill!" yelled Mary above the noise of the crowd. Her dark eyes smiled warmly at him. "Let's run for it!"

Catherine watched as the couple jumped from the truck and ran, laughing, arm in arm, into the crowd.

Soon the police came back with new troops and new meat trucks, and they cleared the street. But Freddie Drummond never came back. In the years that followed he gave no more lectures at the University of California. But a new labor leader rose to fame, named William Totts. He married Mary Condon in a simple ceremony and together they lived for many years, south of The Slot.

Reading Comprehension

1. The people of San Francisco called Market Street "The Slot" because
   a. it divided the rich from the poor sections of the city.
   b. cable car tracks ran down the middle of Market Street.
   c. it was always jammed with traffic.
2. Freddie Drummond was comfortable on both sides of Market Street because
   a. he often lived as a working man south of Market while he was writing his books, which made him famous among the wealthy of Nob Hill.
   b. his books were read by both rich and poor people.
   c. he could easily live anywhere.
3. Freddie Drummond liked to dance, drink, and go on picnics with girls
   a. when he was a student in college.
   b. when he socialized with fashionable Nob Hill society.
   c. when he lived south of The Slot, pretending he was Big Bill Totts.
4. When Freddie Drummond crossed south of The Slot,
   a. he changed his personality as easily as he changed his clothes.
   b. he always got stuck in a traffic jam.
   c. he was running away from his fiancée.
5. "Big" Bill Totts first met Mary Condon when
   a. Professor Drummond sent him to investigate the Laundry Strike.
   b. he was working as a teamster and was sent to a Mission Street boarding house.
   c. her father, a professor at the university, introduced them.

6. Freddie Drummond decided he would marry Catherine Van Vorst so that
   a. Bill Totts could not marry Mary Condon.
   b. he could spend her father's money.
   c. he could write a book about aristocratic women.
7. Freddie Drummond thought he would never see Mary Condon again when
   a. she found out he was engaged to Catherine.
   b. the police took her away.
   c. he and Catherine were caught in a riot on Market Street.
8. When Catherine saw her fiancé leap out of her car and punch a policeman,
   a. she joined in the riot too.
   b. she realized they would never get married.
   c. she watched with amazement.

Vocabulary Check

Choose the sentence below that is closest in meaning to the model.

1. The Slot symbolized the class distinctions of society.
   a. Market Street divided the poor and rich sections of San Francisco.
   b. Many classrooms were located on Market Street.
   c. Market Street was the scene of many working-class battles.
2. Freddie Drummond learned how to do a very good imitation of a genuine worker.
   a. Freddie could understand the language of the workers.
   b. Freddie learned how to do the workers' jobs.
   c. Freddie learned how to talk and act like a typical worker.
3. If he wanted to, he could cross The Slot any time and easily fit into life south of Market.
   a. He could go into the working-class district any time he wished and feel comfortable.
   b. He could wear working-class clothes, which fit him comfortably, any time he wished.
   c. He had to decide if he wanted to live south of Market Street.
4. Drummond had no vices, nor had he discovered any temptations.
   a. Freddie didn't have any bad habits or girl friends.
   b. Freddie didn't have any bad habits, or even any desire to do anything bad.
   c. Freddie never had fun in Berkeley.
5. If Drummond had a woman of his own kind, he wouldn't think about Mary Condon so much.
   a. He wanted to get his own girl friend so he wouldn't be tempted to steal Bill Tott's.
   b. He wanted to own Mary Condon.
   c. He wanted a girl friend from his own class, so he could forget about Mary Condon.

6. Since he was not by nature a polygamist, he was frightened by the possibilities.
   a. He didn't believe that a man should have more than one wife, so he was afraid of loving both Mary Condon and Catherine Van Vorst.
   b. He wasn't a good fighter, so he was afraid Mary Condon and Catherine Van Vorst would beat him up.
   c. He was naturally afraid of women, so he never introduced Catherine Van Vorst to Mary Condon.
7. The moment he recognized Mary, he became Bill Totts.
   a. As soon as he saw Mary, he remembered Bill Totts.
   b. As soon as he saw Mary, he ran into Bill Totts.
   c. As soon as he saw Mary, he changed into Bill Totts.

Story Summary

By answering the following questions, you will write a paragraph that summarizes the story.

Who was Freddie Drummond? Why did he live among the poor people south of Market Street? After working for a while south of The Slot, how did Professor Drummond change? Who was Bill Totts and how was he different from Freddie Drummond? What are some examples of things Bill Totts did south of The Slot that Freddie Drummond would never have done? Who was Mary Condon and why was Freddie afraid to cross south of The Slot after he fell in love with her? Why did Drummond decide to marry Catherine Van Vorst? Compare Catherine with Mary. When did Freddie change his mind about marrying Catherine? How does the story end?

Analyzing the Text

In "South of The Slot," Jack London creates the illusion of two distinct characters: Freddie Drummond and Bill Totts, but these two are really the same man. Carefully reread the story to examine how the author accomplishes this trick.

1. In the beginning of the story, the reader meets Professor Drummond. In which paragraph is "Big" Bill Totts first introduced?
2. As the story continues, London compares Totts and Drummond by describing what they do and how they think. Use different colored pens or markers to highlight or underline the clauses describing each man. Note that most paragraphs that discuss one man also refer to the other

half of this dual-personality character. For most of the story, the professor and the working man are closely connected to each other.

It was as if Freddie Drummond and Bill Totts were totally different people. While he was on the job, <u>Bill Totts worked as slowly as possible</u>, **chatting** with the girls until a **foreman** caught him and sent him back to work. On the other hand *Freddie Drummond condemned lazy workers as un-American,* unproductive, and unpatriotic. *Freddie Drummond did not enjoy dancing,* but <u>Big Bill Totts never missed a night at the Flamingo Dance Hall</u>, where he won first prize as best dancer at the Butchers' and Meatworkers' Annual Grand Masked Ball. Bill Totts liked the girls and the girls liked him, but Freddie Drummond had few female friends and felt uncomfortable when talking with the young women in his university classes.

3. But as the story ends, what happens to Freddie Drummond? Once the scene changes to the labor riot on Market Street and Freddie sees Mary Condon, how does Jack London make the reader clearly see that Freddie is disappearing and "Big" Bill is taking over his life?

Grammar and Sentence Writing

Using *When* and *While* to Combine Sentences

When two sentences are related because the actions occurred at the same *time*, they can be combined by using *when* or *while* to form a subordinate clause:

He lived and worked south of Market for six months.
He was writing a book about the workers in the factories.

He lived and worked south of Market for six months, *while* he was writing a book about the workers in the factories.

Remember that a simple clause beginning with *when* or *while* is not a complete sentence but must be joined to another, independent, clause.

He was writing a book about the workers in the factories.

The sentence above is complete, but when a subordinate conjunction like *when* is added, the clause must be connected to an independent clause.

When he first crossed Market Street, . . . (What happened then?)

The above subordinate clause cannot stand alone as a sentence, but must be joined to an independent clause:

he had a hard time making friends.

The complete complex sentence would read:

When he first crossed Market Street, he had a hard time making friends.

Use *while* to subordinate a continuing action that begins before the action described in the independent clause:

While I was slicing the turkey I cut my finger.

When can be used to subordinate either clause of a complex sentence that combines ideas related in time:

I was slicing the turkey when I cut my finger.

Reread the story, looking for sentences using *when* or *while* as in the examples above.

Sentence Combining

Combine the following sentences as shown in the models below.

MODEL:
He kept a notebook of the workers' slang.
He was working with them. (while)

He kept a notebook of the workers' slang while he was working

with them.

MODEL:
His second book was published. (when)
Freddie Drummond became a celebrity.

When his second book was published, Freddie Drummond became

a celebrity.

1. They were given holidays away from work. (when)
   They would only get drunk and into fights.

   _____

   _____

2. He was a student in college. (while)
   He never socialized with friends.

   _____

   _____

3. He was afraid his companions would discover his true identity. (when) His wild behavior had been only to show them that he was a typical laborer.

   _____

   _____

4. He dreamed of his next adventure south of The Slot.
   He was in Berkeley. (when)

   _____

   _____

5. He was on the job. (while)
   Bill Totts worked as slowly as possible.

   _____

   _____

6. Freddie Drummond changed his clothes. (when)
   He changed his manners too.

   _____

   _____

7. The Longshoremen's Union called a strike. (when)
   He was there with the strikers on the picket line.

   _____

   _____

8. He was collecting information for a third book. (while)
   Bill Totts fell in love.

   _____

   _____

9. He had first seen her at a union meeting.
   She was giving a rousing speech. (when)

   _____

   _____

10. He was working as a delivery truck driver. (while)
    Totts was called to remove a trunk from a boarding house.

    _____

    _____

11. Mary had stopped by to pay the rent.
    She saw Big Bill struggling with the heavy load. (when)

    _____

    _____

12. Totts arrived and saw Mary. (when)
    He forgot all about Freddie Drummond.

    _____

    _____

13. Freddie Drummond announced his engagement to Catherine. (when)
    Everyone thought it would be a wise marriage.

    _____

    _____

14. Freddie Drummond had been transformed into Big Bill Totts.
    He saw Mary Condon battling the police. (when)

    _____

    _____

    _____

Sentence Completion

Using the clauses below, add your own words to form complete sentences. Write *the entire sentence* in the space provided.

MODEL:
While Freddie and Catherine were driving to the florist's shop . . .

While Freddie and Catherine were driving to the florist shop, they

got stuck in a traffic jam.

1. Bill Totts was removing a trunk from a Mission Street boarding house
   when . . .

   _____

   _____

2. Freddie decided to marry Catherine when . . .

   _____

   _____

   _____

3. Bill Totts had fallen in love while . . .

_____

_____

4. When Freddie Drummond crossed south of The Slot, . . .

_____

_____

5. While Catherine watched the battle between strikers and police, . . .

_____

_____

6. When Freddie recognized Mary atop the coal truck, . . .

_____

_____

Conditional Sentences

Complex sentences with _if_ are used to describe what will, may, or can happen _if_ something else happens.

If Freddie sees Mary again, he will never go back.

Complex sentences have two subjects and two verb phrases. In the sentence above, the subject of the dependent or _if_ clause is _Freddie,_ and the verb phrase is _sees._ In the independent clause the subject is _he_ and the verb phrase is _will never go back._ When the verb in the _if_ clause is in the simple present tense, _will, may,_ or _can_ must be used in the independent clause.

The sentence above expresses a probable or possible condition, because there is a good chance that this will really happen—that if Freddie sees Mary, he will stay south of The Slot and never go back to Berkeley. A second kind of conditional sentence can be written to express an idea or event that cannot or probably will not happen.

If Mary knew who Bill really was, she would not love him.

The past tense is used in the _if_ clause even though the action that will not take place is in the present or future. _Would, could,_ or _might_ are always used in the independent clause when the verb in the _if_ clause is in the past tense.

It's important to recognize the difference between the two conditions. For example, which answer means you have a good chance of getting a loan?

I will loan you the money if I can. *OR*
I would loan you the money if I could.

In formal English, *were* is always used in place of was in the *if* clause.

If I *were* you, I would not tell her.
If Mary *were* here, she would tell him.

Writing Conditional Sentences

Positive Conditionals   **Rewrite the following sentences as shown in the models below.**

MODEL:
If he wants to, he can easily fit into life south of Market.

If he wanted to, he could easily fit into life south of Market.

MODEL:
If they are given the chance, they will steal anything they can.

If they were given the chance, they would steal anything they could.

1. "If you're in the union, you'll have a union card."

_____

_____

2. "If you come down to the truck, I'll show it to you."

_____

_____

3. If he has a woman of his own kind, he won't think about Mary Condon so much.

_____

_____

4. If Freddie Drummond doesn't get married, Bill Totts surely will.

_____

_____

5. He doesn't know what Bill Totts will do if he crosses south of Market.

_____

_____

6. If the meat companies deliver meat to the big hotels, they can break the strike.

_____

_____

7. If she screams and holds him tightly, he will understand her fear.

_____

_____

Negative Conditionals   **Rewrite the following sentences as shown in the models below.**

MODEL:

I'm not as big as you, so I can't push that big fat boss out of the way.

If I were as big as you, I could push that big fat boss out of

the way.

MODEL:

The coal truck won't move, so the police can't proceed.

If the coal truck would move, the police could proceed.

1. The police can't get the driver out, so they can't move the truck themselves.

_____

_____

2. He doesn't have a woman of his own kind, so he thinks about Mary Condon all the time.

_____

_____

3. He is carrying the heavy trunk, so he can't get his union card out of his pocket.

_____

_____

4. Mary won't come down to the truck, so he can't show her his union card.

_____

_____

5. Freddie Drummond isn't as friendly as Bill Totts, so he doesn't have as many friends.

_____

_____

_____

6. Mary Condon doesn't know that Bill Totts is really a university professor, so she trusts him.

_____

_____

Word Forms

Choose the correct word to complete each sentence below.

society   sociology   sociological   antisocial

1. Because Freddie Drummond had few friends, many thought he was

_____.

2. The wealthy of Nob Hill thought they were the upper class of

_____.

3. _____ is the study of society.

4. Freddie Drummond first went south of Market Street to do

_____ research.

violence   violently   violent

1. The _____ mob fought a bloody battle with the police.

2. Professor Drummond wrote that _____ on the picket line should be severely punished.

3. Mary Condon _____ pushed Bill Totts against the wall when he refused to show her his union card.

battled   battling   battle

1. The strikers _____ the police to prevent the meat trucks from supplying the big hotels.

2. When the longshoremen were _____ police on the picket line, Bill Totts was there fighting too.

3. Catherine and Freddie were surprised to find their car stuck in the middle of a _____ between police and striking meat workers.

symbolic   symbol   symbolized

1. Market Street _____ the line dividing rich and poor in San Francisco.

2. Catherine's fine clothes were _____ of her wealth and aristocracy.

3. Bill Totts' working-class cap was a _____ of his new personality.

Comparatives

When comparing two unequal subjects, use the word *more* if the comparative adjective has three syllables or more.

> **Nob Hill is *more aristocratic* than the Mission District.**

A/ris/to/crat/ic has five syllables, so use *more*.

> **Poor people are *happier* than the aristocrats.**

Hap/py has only two syllables, so add *-er* to form a comparative. (Note that when you change *happy* to *happier* the *y* changes to *i* because it is preceded by a consonant.)

Writing Comparatives

Write sentences using comparatives as shown in the following models.

MODEL:
University professors / rich / factory workers

University professors are richer than factory workers. _____

MODEL:
The rich / comfortable / the poor

The rich are more comfortable than the poor. _____

1. Mary Condon / passionate / Catherine Van Vorst

_____

2. Bill Totts / friendly / Freddie Drummond

_____

3. Catherine / wealthy / Mary

_____

4. People south of Market / poor / people on Nob Hill

_____

5. Bill Totts / good dancer / Freddie Drummond

_____

6. Freddie Drummond / shy / Bill Totts

_____

7. Catherine / aristocratic / Mary

_____

8. Freddie Drummond / conservative / Bill Totts

_____

9. The houses on Nob Hill / fancy / the houses south of The Slot

_____

10. Mary Condon / wild / Catherine Van Vorst

_____

Developing Ideas

Topics for Discussion

Form a small group with some of your classmates and discuss the following topics.

1. _The Labor Movement_

Jack London writes of a San Francisco divided between rich and poor. The working class was isolated from the rich. Striking workers were attacked by police and soldiers, while the rich believed the poor were an inferior class. Have things changed? Does labor have more power now? Are strikes still common today? Are they still violent? Are the rich and the poor just as isolated from one another today as they were in London's San Francisco? What do you think are the reasons for any such changes?

2. *Social Classes*

Do poor people have more fun than the rich? If not, why did Freddie decide to give up his middle-class life? Compare Mary to Catherine. Whose life is more interesting and exciting? Who is more comfortable? Why couldn't Freddie find a woman like Mary at the university? Are most working women today like Mary Condon? Are most rich women today like Catherine Van Vorst? Are there many types of people who don't fit either *stereotype?* (See For Further Discussion, below.)

3. *Jack London, Socialist*

Jack London sympathized with the poor and disapproved of the wealthy. He grew up in Oakland in a very poor family, never went to college, and knew very little about the rich. What do we learn about his political opinions, biases, and prejudices from reading "South of The Slot"? What does London think about education? Wealthy women? Working-class parties and social parties? The police? Labor unions?

Paragraph Writing

Freddie Drummond

1. What would you do if you were Freddie Drummond? (Begin your paragraph with the sentence "If I were Freddie. . . .") What would you do if you knew two women who wanted to get married? ("If I knew two women who. . . .") Would you give up a good position like the one Freddie Drummond had at the university? ("I would. . . , if. . . .") If you had to choose between Catherine and Mary, which one would you choose? ("If I had to choose, ...") Explain your choice.

Catherine Van Vorst

2. Write a paragraph discussing what you would do if you were Catherine Van Vorst, sitting in her car watching her fiancé run away with a strange woman. Is there anything you could do to get him back? Would you try to find him? What would you tell your friends whom you have already invited to the wedding? Begin your paragraph by writing "If I were Catherine Van Vorst. . . ."

The Picket Line

3. If you saw a picket line in front of the place where you worked, would you cross it? Would you cross a picket line to shop in a store? In each case, explain why you would or would not cross the line of strikers.

Role Playing

A few years have passed since Freddie Drummond disappeared into the crowd on Market Street. Catherine Van Vorst has gone back to her father's home in Berkeley, while Bill Totts and his wife Mary Condon have continued their work in the labor movement. One day, after a busy afternoon of shopping, Catherine is hurrying down Market Street toward the Ferry Building. Because she is carrying a heavy load of shopping bags and packages, Catherine doesn't see the man stopped in front of her. She bumps into him, dropping her bags on the sidewalk. Apologizing, both begin to pick up the fallen packages. When they look up, they immediately recognize each other. Catherine has bumped into Bill Totts, whom she knew as Freddie Drummond! What do you think they would say to each other? Choose a partner and write a dialogue between Catherine and Bill, then act it out in front of the class. You might begin as suggested below:

> **Bill Totts/Freddie Drummond:** Oh, Excuse me, ma'am!
> **Catherine:** My goodness, can't you watch where you're walking!
> **Freddie/Bill:** Well, I wasn't walking, lady. I was just standing here.
>   . . . Oh! Catherine! How are you?
> **Catherine:** Oh my God! It's Freddie Drummond!
> **Bill/Freddie:** . . .
> **Catherine:** . . .

For Further Discussion: Stereotypes

Catherine Van Vorst and Mary Condon are *stereotypes,* or individuals whose behavior and appearance are supposedly typical of members of their groups. Thus, most people expect a working-class woman like Mary to be more emotional and outgoing than an aristocratic woman like Catherine. Even Freddie Drummond's behavior is stereotypical. As a professor, he is more interested in studying than socializing, but when he becomes Bill Totts, he is more fun-loving. Are most rich women really like Catherine, and most working-class women like Mary Condon? Is Freddie Drummond a typical professor? Why do stereotypes exist? Is there much truth to them? Stereotypes exist for every ethnic and social group. What are common stereotypes for ethnic groups or nationalities represented in your English class? Discuss among the class the validity of these generalizations and their effects on individuals who are not, and do not wish to be, like the stereotyped image of their group.

The Gift of
the Magi

O. HENRY

The title of this story refers to the Three Wise Men, or Magi, of the Bible who, following a mysterious star, were led to the baby Jesus. According to the New Testament, they offered gifts of gold, frankincense, and myrrh. These were valuable presents but not very useful to a newborn baby. After reading the story, think about why O. Henry named it "The Gift of the Magi." How can the gifts given to the baby Jesus two thousand years ago be compared with the gifts Jim and Della exchange?

THE AUTHOR

At the turn of the twentieth century, William Sydney Porter, using the pen name O. Henry, wrote hundreds of stories enjoyed by millions of Americans. But the author lived a tragic life. He first found success as a writer while a prisoner in a federal penitentiary in Ohio. After he was released, he went to New York where "The Gift of the Magi" was originally published in 1905. It is just one of many sentimental stories he wrote that entertained readers of the daily newspapers of that time, the struggling citizens of the growing city of New York, like his characters Jim and Della. But the writer's success only lasted eight years. At the age of forty-eight, he died of alcoholism.

THE STORY

This is a Christmas story about giving gifts to someone we love:
When we love someone, what is more important, the gift we
give, or the gift we receive?
This is a romantic story about the value of love: What is
more valuable, the love shared by this poor, newly married
couple, Jim and Della, or all the money in New York City
that they do not have?

One dollar and eighty-seven cents. That was all. And sixty cents of it was in pennies. Three times Della counted it. One dollar and eighty-seven cents. And the next day would be Christmas.

worn and faded

Della felt so bad she sat down on their **shabby** little couch and cried, but that didn't help either. Drying her eyes, she walked to the window of the small apartment. The furnished **flat** at eight dollars per week was all that she and her husband Jim could afford on his weekly salary of twenty dollars.

upstairs apartment

But tomorrow would be Christmas Day, and she had only $1.87 with which to buy Jim a present. She had been saving every penny she could for months, with this result. Twenty dollars a week doesn't go far. Expenses had been greater than she had calculated. They always are. Only $1.87 to buy a present for her Jim. She had spent many a happy hour planning to buy something nice for him. If she had only been able to save more money, she could have bought something fine and rare, something that deserved the honor of being owned by Jim.

turning or spinning

Whirling from the window, she stood before the mirror. Her eyes were shining brilliantly, but her face had lost its color. Rapidly she pulled down her hair and let it fall to its full length.

Now, there were two possessions of the James Dillingham Youngs in which they both took great pride. One was Jim's gold watch that had been his father's and his grandfather's. The other was Della's hair.

flowing in small waves

waterfall

article of clothing

Della's beautiful hair fell about her, **rippling** and shining like a **cascade** of brown water. It reached below her knee and made it-self almost a **garment** for her. Then she did it up again nervously and quickly. Once she stopped for a minute and stood still while a tear or two splashed on the worn red carpet.

flashing light

She quickly put on her old brown jacket and her old brown hat. With a whirl of skirts and with the brilliant **sparkle** still in her eyes, she ran out the door and down the stairs to the street.

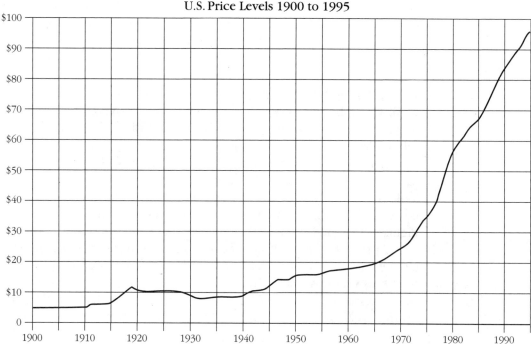

Inflation in the United States since 1900: The graph shows how many dollars would be needed in any year to buy an item that sold for $5 in 1900.

She walked down the street until she saw a sign which read: "Madam Sofronie. Hair Goods of All Kinds. Second Floor." Della ran up the stairs, arriving at the top **panting**. Entering the small shop on the second floor, she was greeted by a large, pale lady.

"Will you buy my hair?" asked Della.

"I buy hair," said Madame. "Take your hat off and let's have a look at it."

Down rippled the brown cascade.

"Twenty dollars," said Madame, lifting the mass with a practiced hand.

"Give it to me quick," said Della.

She passed the next two hours **ecstatically**, searching the stores for Jim's present.

She found it at last. It surely had been made for Jim and no one else. There was no other like it in any of the stores, and she had **turned all of them inside out**. It was a platinum watch chain, simple and clean in design, but of **obvious** quality. As soon as she saw it, she knew that it must be Jim's. She had often seen Jim look at his watch secretly because he didn't want anyone to

breathing quickly

very happily and excitedly

looked thoroughly through every store / easy to see, unmistakable

see the old leather strap that he used in place of a chain. If Jim had had that chain on his watch, he would have been proud to check the time in any company. They took twenty-one dollars from her for the chain, and she hurried home with the eighty-seven cents change.

Reaching home, Della got out her curling irons and went to work fixing her short hair. Soon her head was covered with tiny, close-lying curls that made her look wonderfully like a young schoolgirl.

Looking at her reflection in the mirror, she said to herself, "If Jim doesn't kill me before he takes a second look at me, he'll say I look like a Coney Island chorus girl. But what could I do—oh! what could I do with a dollar and eighty-seven cents? I had to cut my hair. If I hadn't cut it, I wouldn't have been able to buy Jim a present."

At seven o'clock the coffee was made and the frying pan was on the back of the stove, hot and ready to cook the chops.

Jim was never late. **Clutching** the watch chain in her hand, Della sat on the corner of the table near the door. Hearing his step on the stair, she turned white for just a moment. Remembering her short hair, she whispered, "Please, God, make him think I am still pretty."

The door opened and Jim stepped in. He looked thin and very serious. Poor fellow, he was only twenty-two—and to be **burdened** with a family! He needed a new overcoat, and he was without gloves.

Stopping inside the door, he fixed his eyes on Della, and there was an expression in them that she could not read, and it **terrified** her. It was not anger, nor surprise, nor disapproval, nor horror. He simply stared at her with a **peculiar** expression on his face.

Running up to him, Della cried, "Jim, darling, don't look at me that way. I had my hair cut off and sold it because I couldn't have lived through Christmas if I hadn't given you a present. I just had to do it. It'll grow out again—you won't mind, will you? My hair grows awfully fast. Say 'Merry Christmas!' Jim, and let's be happy. You don't know what a nice—what a beautiful, nice gift I've got for you."

"You've cut off your hair?" asked Jim.

"Cut it off and sold it," said Della. "Don't you like me just as well, anyhow? I'm me without my hair, **ain't** I?"

Jim looked about the room curiously.

"You say your hair is gone?" he said, with an air almost of idiocy.

"You needn't look for it," said Della. "It's sold, I tell you—sold and gone, too. It's Christmas Eve, darling. Be good to me. Maybe the hairs of my head were numbered," she went on with a sudden seri-

---

holding tightly

loaded or oppressed
with a heavy weight

frightened

strange

(nonstandard) am not

ous sweetness, "but nobody could ever count my love for you. Shall I put the chops on, Jim?"

Jim seemed to wake out of his **trance,** quickly **hugging** his Della. He drew a package from his overcoat pocket and threw it upon the table.

"Don't make any mistake, Dell," he said, "about me. I don't think there's anything in the way of a haircut or a shave or a shampoo that could make me love you any less. But if you'll unwrap that package, you may see why I was so **startled.**"

Ripping open the package, Della screamed with joy when she saw the present it contained. But then her cry of joy quickly changed to **hysterical** sobs as she held her husband's gift.

There lay the set of combs that Della had **worshipped** for so long in a Broadway window. They were expensive combs, she knew, and her heart had simply **craved** and **yearned** over them without the least hope of possession. And now they were hers, but the long **tresses** that they were meant for were gone now.

Hugging them to her **bosom,** at length she was able to look up with dim eyes and a smile and say: "My hair grows so fast, Jim! I'm sorry I cut it. I would never have done it if I had known you were giving me the combs, but I had to because . . . Oh, Oh!"

Remembering her present, Della jumped up and held it out to him eagerly in her open hand.

"Isn't it a **dandy,** Jim? I hunted all over town to find it. You'll have to look at your watch a hundred times a day now. Give it to me. I want to see how it looks with the chain on it."

Instead of obeying, Jim **tumbled** down on the couch and put his hands behind his head and smiled.

"Dell," said he, "let's put our Christmas presents away and keep 'em a while. They're too nice to use just now. I sold the watch to get the money to buy your combs. And now suppose you put the chops on."

Marginal glossary:

trance, hugging — deep dream or state of hypnosis / holding in one's arms affectionately

startled — surprised

hysterical — very excited, out of control / adored, admired excessively

craved, yearned — wanted desperately / longed for

tresses — long, loose hair

bosom — breast

dandy — (informal) fine, of very good quality

tumbled — fell violently or awkwardly

Reading Comprehension

1. At the beginning of the story, Della was crying because
    a. Jim was late for dinner.
    b. she didn't have enough money to buy him a nice Christmas present.
    c. she couldn't afford Christmas dinner.

2. Della cut her hair because
   a. it was the new style.
   b. Jim didn't like long hair.
   c. she wanted to sell it to buy a present for Jim.
3. Jim and Della were poor because
   a. Jim was very young and had a small salary.
   b. Jim spent their money foolishly.
   c. their rent was too expensive.
4. The young couple were proud of Jim's watch because
   a. it was the finest watch in New York.
   b. it had belonged to his father and his grandfather.
   c. Jim's boss had given it to him.
5. When Jim saw that Della had cut her hair, he was
   a. angry.
   b. surprised.
   c. shocked into a trance.
6. Jim was startled by Della's short hair because
   a. he thought she looked ugly.
   b. he didn't recognize her.
   c. he had already bought the combs for her hair.
7. Jim didn't have his watch because
   a. someone had stolen it.
   b. he had lost it.
   c. he had sold it to buy the combs for Della.
8. When he found out that Della had cut her hair, Jim was
   a. angry that he had sold his watch for nothing.
   b. glad that she had done something to improve her appearance.
   c. happy that they loved each other so much, and hungry.

Vocabulary Check

Choose the sentence that is closest in meaning to the model.

1. Twenty dollars a week doesn't go far.
   a. You can't travel far in a week with only twenty dollars.
   b. Twenty dollars a week is very little money.
   c. Next week is far away.
2. She stood still while a tear splashed on the carpet.
   a. She was standing still, crying.
   b. She spilled wine on the carpet.
   c. She tore the carpet.
3. Della turned the stores inside out looking for a present for Jim.
   a. Della made a big mess in the stores, throwing things around.
   b. Della turned to go inside the stores.
   c. Della looked carefully through many stores.

4. Jim was only twenty-two, but he was already burdened with a family.
   a. He had to carry his children on his back.
   b. He didn't like his family.
   c. He was responsible for taking care of his family.
5. I don't think there's anything in the way of a haircut or a shave or a shampoo that could make me love you any less.
   a. There isn't anything you can do to your hair that will make me stop loving you.
   b. If you went to the barber shop, I would still love you.
   c. I love the way you take care of my hair.
6. The combs were hers, but the long tresses that they were meant for were gone now.
   a. The combs really belonged to someone who had already gone.
   b. She had the combs, but didn't have long hair to put them in.
   c. She combed her long hair after he had gone.
7. I would never have done it if I had known you were giving me the combs.
   a. If I had the combs I would do my hair differently.
   b. I didn't know you were giving me combs, so I cut my hair.
   c. I cut my hair so I could comb it more easily.
8. And now suppose you put the chops on.
   a. Would you like to start cooking the meat now?
   b. I guess you should chop up the meat.
   c. Why do you always cook chops?

Analyzing the Text

What Does "Love" Mean?

Love is word that can mean many things. "The Gift of the Magi" is a story about the kind of love that a young wife feels for her husband. But how can such a powerful emotion be described? First O. Henry tells us what Della *does* to demonstrate her love for Jim. Then we read what she *says* to herself and to Jim, and we can judge her love by her words.

In the lines below, write examples of Della's actions and speech that demonstrate her love for Jim.

What did Della **do** that shows her love for Jim?

MODEL:
She cut off her long hair.

1. _____

2. _____

3. _____

What did Della **say** that shows her love for Jim?

MODEL:

She said that she was worried that Jim would not like her short hair.

1. _____

2. _____

3. _____

Interpreting Graphs

The graph on page 57 of this story illustrates U.S. price levels from 1900 to 1995. It shows inflation of the cost of living, mea-sured in dollars. Study the graph to find the information you need to answer the following questions:

1. How much is five dollars in 1900 worth today? If today's dollar had the same value as it did in 1900, how much could you buy with five dollars?
2. Jim's office job paid twenty dollars per week. Convert that amount into today's dollars. Are wages higher today, or about the same?
3. Della and Jim paid eight dollars a week to rent their flat in New York City. How much would that be in today's dollars? Were rents cheaper a hundred years ago?
4. Usually, the cost of living has risen, as can be seen by the rising line of the graph. But between 1920 and 1940 prices did not increase. Instead of inflation, there was even some deflation in prices. What happened to the economy to cause this?

Grammar and Sentence Writing

Participial Phrases

Della and Jim lived in New York.
The young couple could only afford a small apartment.

Two simple sentences sharing the same subject can be joined together by changing one sentence into a participial phrase. Change the verb to a present principle (ending in -*ing*):

Living in New York, the young couple could only afford a small apartment.

The participial phrase can be placed after the main clause. The following simple sentences can be combined as shown below:

Della ran into the department store.
She was thinking about Jim's present.

Della ran into the department store, *thinking* of Jim's present.

Reread the story looking for sentences containing participial phrases.

Sentence Writing A

MODEL:
Della dried her eyes. She walked to the window of the small apartment.

Drying her eyes, Della walked to the window of the small apartment.

MODEL:
Della whirled from the window. She stood before the mirror.

Whirling from the window, Della stood before the mirror.

1. Della's beautiful hair fell about her. It rippled and shone like a cascade of brown water.

2. She entered the small shop on the second floor. She was greeted by a large, pale lady.

3. She looked at her reflection in the mirror. She said to herself, "I hope Jim doesn't kill me!"

4. Della clutched the watch chain in her hand. She sat on the corner of the table near the door.

5. She heard his steps on the stair. She turned white for just a moment.

   _____

   _____

6. She suddenly remembered her short hair. She whispered, "Please, God, make him think I am still pretty."

   _____

   _____

7. He stopped inside the door. He fixed his eyes on Della.

   _____

   _____

8. She ran up to him. She cried, "Jim, darling, don't look at me that way."

   _____

   _____

9. Jim seemed to wake out of his trance. He quickly hugged his Della.

   _____

   _____

10. Della ripped open the package. She screamed with joy when she saw the present it contained.

    _____

    _____

11. She hugged the combs to her bosom. At length she was able to look up at her husband.

    _____

    _____

12. Della hoped to buy her husband a fine present for Christmas. She had been saving all the money she could.

    _____

    _____

13. Della looked out the window. She saw a grey cat in a grey yard.

    _____

    _____

14. Jim opened the door. He saw Della waiting for him.

_____

_____

Sentence Completion

Using the phrases below, add your own words to form complete sentences. Write the *entire sentence* in the space provided.

1. Opening the door, Jim . . .

_____

_____

2. Waiting for Jim to come home from work, Della . . .

_____

_____

3. She looked at her hair in the mirror, thinking . . .

_____

_____

4. Seeing his wife with short hair for the first time, Jim . . .

_____

_____

5. Opening the package, Della . . .

_____

_____

Sentence Writing B

Answer the following questions with complete sentences. In your answer, write two clauses, connected with *because, so, when,* or *while.*

1. Why was Della saving money?

_____

_____

2. While looking at her hair in the mirror, what did Della decide to do?

_____

_____

3. Where did Della go after selling her hair?

_____

_____

4. After buying the watch chain, what did Della do to her short hair before Jim came home?

_____

_____

5. What did Jim do upon first seeing his wife with short hair?

_____

_____

6. Why couldn't Jim use the watch chain Della had bought him?

_____

_____

7. Why did Jim sell his most valuable possession?

_____

_____

8. Why weren't Jim and Della sad or angry when they each realized that the other person had given up the most valuable thing he or she owned?

_____

_____

Past Conditional Sentences

In "The Gift of the Magi," Jim and Della give each other Christmas presents which they *would not have given* if they *had known* what they were going to receive. O. Henry makes the reader think about what they *might have done* to demonstrate their love for each other instead of buying presents they could not afford.

When language is used to express ideas that are contrary to reality, or events did not happen, verbs are used differently:

> *Would* the couple *have been* happier if they *had not sold* their most treasured possessions to buy useless presents?

> *Could* Jim *have enjoyed* his new watch chain if he *had not sold* his watch, or *would* he *have felt* very sad because he *had not given* his wife a fancy present?

These are *past conditional sentences,* describing events in the past which did not happen. They are based on a condition, stated in the *if* clause, that is unreal.

> *If* Jim *had been* rich, (he wasn't rich)
>   he *could have bought* Della anything.

Reread "The Gift of the Magi" and find all the "if" sentences that follow this pattern:

> *If* (subject) *had* + past principle, (subject) *could have* + past participle.

with:

                                                                 would
                                                                 should

Reread the story to find five past conditional sentences like those above. Underline the verb phrases in each clause of each sentence you find. Not all begin with *if.* The *if* clause may follow the main clause.

Writing Past Conditional Sentences A

Adding your own words, form complete sentences using the clauses below. Write the entire sentence in the space provided.

1. If Della had known that Jim had sold the watch, . . .

_____

_____

2. If the couple had been rich, . . .

_____

_____

3. Della would have been happy to receive the combs if . . .

_____

_____

4. Jim and Della would have been happier if . . .

_____

_____

5. If all married couples loved each other as much as Jim and Della, . . .

_____

_____

_____

6. Last Christmas, if I could have gotten anything I wanted, . . .

_____

_____

Writing Past Conditional Sentences B

In the space provided, write the answers to the following questions in complete sentences. Include the _if_ clause in each answer.

1. Would Della have cut her hair if she had been wealthy?

_____

_____

2. If Jim had known that Della was going to buy him a watch chain, would he have sold his watch?

_____

_____

3. Could Della have saved more money for Jim's present if he had earned more than twenty dollars a week?

_____

_____

4. Would Jim and Della have been happier if they had not bought anything for each other?

_____

_____

5. If they had given each other handmade gifts, how would the story have ended?

_____

_____

6. What would you have said if your husband or wife had sold his or her most valuable possession to buy you a present?

_____

_____

Guided Paragraph Writing

Sample Paragraph A   My name is Della Young. I am married to Jim, a wonderful man whom I love very much. Last Christmas I did a very foolish thing. Because I didn't have enough money to buy my husband an expensive Christmas gift, I sold my long hair to buy him a platinum chain for his gold watch. But I didn't know that Jim had already sold his watch so that he could buy me a fine present. He bought me combs for my long hair! If I had known that Jim was going to give me combs, I would not have cut my hair. Also, I would not have bought Jim a chain for his watch if I had known that he had sold it. If we had given each other inexpensive gifts, we would have been just as happy, and we still would have owned our two most treasured possessions—Jim's watch and my beautiful hair.

Writing Assignment   After reading Della's paragraph, above, write your own paragraph in which you describe a past mistake of your own. Write about a decision you made, or something you did, that you would have changed if you had known better. When writing about what you might have done to avoid the mistake, use past conditional *if* sentences. Explain how things would have been different if you had not made this mistake.

Sample Paragraph B   My name is John Fitzgerald Kennedy. I was elected President of the United States in 1960. On November 22, 1963, I flew from Washington D.C. to Dallas, Texas. While riding in a parade through the city, I was shot and killed. If I had ridden in a bulletproof car, I would not have died. I believe that I could have made the United States a better country if I had lived. If I had not been assassinated, I could have been a great leader and I could have watched my children grow up. If I had never gone to Dallas, the world would be a better place today.

Writing Assignment   After reading the above statement, write a paragraph in which you pretend to be a famous person in history who suffered a tragic defeat or embarrassment. You could be Napoleon, Marie Antoinette, Richard Nixon, the Shah of Iran, Princess Diana, or anyone else you choose. Explain what you might have done differently to change your life. Begin with the sentence "My name is . . . ." Explain how the world would have been different if you had only done something differently.

Sample Paragraph C   I was not born in Jamaica, but if I had been born there, I would have been a happy baby. I could have eaten pineapples, bananas, and papayas instead of baby food. If my mother had been Jamaican, she would have taught me to speak English, so I would not have had to take this class. But best of all, if I had grown up in Jamaica, I would have learned how to swim, because the warm Caribbean Sea surrounds that island.

Writing Assignment   After reading the sample paragraph, above, pick any country you wish and write a paragraph beginning: "I was not born in _____, but if I had been born there, I would have been a happy baby." Explain why you would have been happy there as a child. How would life have been different for you? Compare your fantasy childhood with your real childhood. What new experiences would you have enjoyed in the country of your choice? What would you have missed if you had not grown up in your native country?

Writing Comparatives

Choosing the correct form of comparison, write sentences as shown in the models below:

MODEL:
James Dillingham Young's watch / valuable / possession he owned

James Dillingham Young's watch was the most valuable possession

he owned.

MODEL:
His wife's love / important / his watch

His wife's love was more important than his watch.

_____

MODEL:
Della's hair / short / than it had been that morning

Della's hair was shorter than it had been that morning.

MODEL:
When she found out that Jim had sold his watch, Della / startled / he was when he saw her hair

Della was as startled as he was when he saw her hair.

1. Della loved Jim / much / Jim loved Della

_____

_____

_____

2. Jim and Della / poor / Catherine Van Vorst

———————————————————————————————

———————————————————————————————

3. The cost of living in 1900 / high / today

———————————————————————————————

———————————————————————————————

4. Platinum watch chain / valuable / old leather strap

———————————————————————————————

———————————————————————————————

5. Della / happy / Catherine Van Vorst

———————————————————————————————

———————————————————————————————

6. Salaries today / large / in 1900

———————————————————————————————

———————————————————————————————

7. Jim and Della / loved each other / Mary Condon and Bill Totts

———————————————————————————————

———————————————————————————————

8. The combs / beautiful / she had ever seen

———————————————————————————————

———————————————————————————————

9. Love / important / money

———————————————————————————————

———————————————————————————————

10. The working class in New York / poor / workers in San Francisco

———————————————————————————————

———————————————————————————————

11. In 1900 O. Henry / popular writer / today

———————————————————————————————

———————————————————————————————

12. "The Gift of the Magi" / good story / "South of the Slot"

_____

_____

13. O. Henry / popular writer / in New York City in 1900

_____

_____

14. Jim believed that Della / good wife / a man could have

_____

_____

Developing Ideas

Topics for Discussion

Form a small group with some of your classmates and discuss the following topics:

1. The Nature of Giving

How does "The Gift of the Magi" compare the joy of giving with the joy of receiving? Explain why Della and Jim are happy at the end of the story, even after sacrificing their most treasured possessions. Since their presents for each other are useless, wouldn't it have been wiser for them to have simply not bought anything for each other? What do their gifts show about their relationship? Would you rather give or receive? Does it make a difference if you exchange gifts with someone you love very much or with a casual friend? Does a good gift have to be expensive? Why?

2. The Custom of Giving Gifts at Christmas

In the United States, most people exchange gifts at Christmas. Is this true everywhere? In countries where Christmas is not celebrated, are there other holidays when gifts are exchanged? Is Christmas a religious holiday? Why do people give gifts to each other? Do other religions celebrate religious holidays in a similar manner? It seems the first Christmas presents were given by the Magi, described in the New Testament of the Bible. Were their gifts any more useful to the baby Jesus than were Jim and Della's gifts to each other? Why did O. Henry choose this title for his story?

3. Inflation

When money loses value as time goes on, people worry about inflation. O. Henry wrote "The Gift of the Magi" in 1905 for *The World,* a New York City newspaper. Jim and Della are a poor young couple. How much does

Jim make each week? How much rent do they pay for a small apartment? How does their salary and rent compare with yours? Do you consider yourself rich or poor? If you had as much money as you have today, how could you have lived in 1905? Is New York City a town where
you can live cheaply? Do you think that eight dollars per week was
considered cheap rent in 1905? What do you think prices will be like in
the future?

Role Playing

Imagine that you are Jim and Della sitting down to eat your pork chops
after you have opened your presents. Carry on a typical dinner-table
conversation. What will you say about your present? If you are Jim,
what can you say about your wife's hair? If you are Della, do you try to
make Jim forget about your hair, or do you talk about how fast it will
grow back and how prettily you can fix short hair? What do you say
about the watch? Are you sorry you sold your most treasured possessions? Can you still have a merry Christmas?

Choose a partner in the class, practice your roles as Jim and Della,
and then act out the Christmas dinner scene. You might begin your conversation as suggested below:

> **Della:** Dinner's ready, Jim!
> **Jim:** I'm so hungry, Della. I love the way you cook pork chops.
> **Della:** I wanted you to have your favorite dinner on Christmas
>   Eve, dear.
> **Jim:** . . .
> **Della:** . . .

For Further Discussion: Irony

Irony is the difference between what *is* and what *is expected*. When a
story ends differently from what the reader had expected, this surprise
ending can be considered *ironic* if the contrast between what *is* and
what *might have been* helps the reader understand the significance or
meaning of the story. The ironic ending of "The Gift of the Magi" not
only helps us to understand the story but also makes it more enjoyable.

Answering the following questions, discuss the ironic twist in
O. Henry's story: When Della gave the watch chain to her husband,
what did she expect him to do with it? Why wasn't Jim able to use the
chain? When Jim gave his wife the combs, how did he think she would
use them, and why was this impossible? Each thought that giving such
an expensive gift would make the other happy. In spite of what they
had done, the couple was happy at the end of the story. Why? What
might they have done with their Christmas presents if they hadn't sold
his watch and her hair? How would this have changed the meaning of
the story?

The Only Rose

SARAH ORNE JEWETT

THE AUTHOR

*Sarah Orne Jewett was born in 1849 in South Berwick, Maine.
She never married, and, although she traveled abroad
frequently with her life-long friend Annie Adams Fields and
was acquainted with many of the well-known British and
American writers of the time, she lived her entire life in this
small New England community. Her writing preserves the lives
of ordinary people of traditional New England society, whom
she came to know as a young woman when she accompanied
her physician father on his visits to local patients. "The Only
Rose" reflects her interest in the lives of the common women of
her time, and the economic and social problems they faced.*

THE STORY

*"The Only Rose" concerns an elderly widow and the
responsibility she still feels toward the three late husbands she
has buried during her long life. In traditional New England,
wives and husbands had clear roles in marriage. One duty of
a wife would be to properly mourn her dead mate and to look
after his grave once he had been buried. The main character,
Mrs. Bickford, was certainly a good widow.
But husbands had clear responsibilities, too. Was the husband
financially responsible for his wife? Even after he died? While
Mrs. Bickford cannot bring herself to judge the three men—she
cannot even choose the grave for "the only rose"—the reader
can decide if the men she married were all good husbands.
Before reading the story, think about the different
responsibilities of husbands and wives, both today and in the
past, when women were treated very differently.*

I

At the edge of Fairfield, just where the village ended and the green
fields began, stood Mrs. Bickford's house. Leaving the road, you could
follow a straight path from the gate past the front door and find
Mrs. Bickford sitting by the last window in the kitchen, unless she
were **solemnly** stepping about doing her **solitary** housekeeping.

    The afternoon sun was pouring in, shining on a large bunch of
freshly cut, brightly colored flowers, when a neighbor, Miss Pendexter, came in from the next house to make a friendly call. As her
neighbor passed through the empty big house into the kitchen, she

seriously, respectfully /
alone

woman whose
husband has died

wished that somebody else beside the **widowed** owner might have
the pleasure of living in such a nice big house. Mrs. Bickford always
complained of having so much to care for, even while she was
proud to live in one of the best houses in Fairfield.

    Miss Pendexter was a cheerful person who always brought a
sudden rush   pleasant **flurry** of excitement, and usually had a small piece of
news to tell, so Mrs. Bickford smiled as she saw her neighbor coming. She was always glad to have a visitor to help pass the day.

    Miss Pendexter smiled back. "How are you today Mrs. Bickford?
I find it hard to believe it's spring already! This year has been going
by so quickly!" she said as she entered the kitchen. "Why, what a
sight of flowers. What are you going to do with them all?"

serious   Mrs. Bickford wore a **grave** expression as she looked over her
glasses. "My sister's boy brought them over," she answered. "You
know my sister is a great gardener, and my nephew takes after her.
He said his mother thought the garden never looked handsomer,

Women Win the Right to Vote

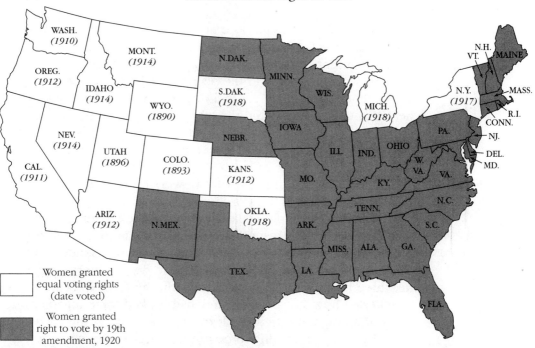

In 1894, when this story was written, American women were second-class citizens. Their rights to work, to own property, and to divorce were controlled by men. The map included here shows the year women were granted equal voting rights in each state.

and she picked these flowers for me." The boy stopped and ate his lunch here. He's been growing fast and looks like a man. I expect my sister 'Liza thought I needed some company. "Liza sent word for me to come over and pass the day tomorrow."

"Why it's a pretty time of year to go off and make a little visit," suggested the neighbor encouragingly.

"I haven't cleaned my living room carpet yet," sighed Mrs. Bickford. "I should have done it today, but when I saw Johnny coming, that was the end of that. He's a nice boy, and what a good eater! I think he's my favorite of that family, but I've been sitting here thinking, since he left, that I have waited far too long to start my spring cleaning."

"It's because of the weather," explained Miss Pendexter. "None of us has gotten anything done but the flowers have surely been growing!"

The two women laughed together cheerfully. Mrs. Bickford had spread out the flowers on her large table and was sorting them slowly into three piles.

Miss Pendexter looked through the open window. "Why, look,

shouted

you have a rose in bloom yourself!" she **exclaimed**. "Isn't it a lovely rose? Why, Mrs. Bickford!"

"Yes'm, it's out today" said Mrs. Bickford, with a somewhat proud air. "I'm glad you've come in so as to see it."

The bright flower was like a face. Somehow, the beauty and life of it were surprising in the plain room, like a happy little child who might suddenly appear in a doorway. Miss Pendexter forgot herself and her hostess and the table full of garden flowers in looking at the red rose. She also forgot that she was engaged in conversation with Mrs. Bickford, who was lost in thought herself, staring at the beauty of the red rose.

bunch of flowers

"Are you going to make your flowers into **bouquets**? They'd look so beautiful, Mrs. Bickford!"

emotion

"I thought I should make them into three bouquets," said Mrs. Bickford with unusual emotion. She normally did not speak with so much **sentiment**, and her neighbor was surprised. Suddenly she realized that the three piles of flowers were destined for the graves of her three husbands, all buried close by in the Fairfield cemetery. Remembering how in past years they had walked there together on pleasant spring days, Miss Pendexter looked again at the pretty rose.

"I guess you're going to carry them over to the burying-ground?" Asked the guest, in a sympathetic tone.

"Yes'm," said the hostess, now in her everyday manner. "You see I decided to go over to my sister's tomorrow like they invited me. Johnny'll come and get me in the morning to take me back, and we'll stop off at the burying ground on the way. I've been wanting to visit the graveyard anyway, so I thought it would be a good opportunity to just stop and see if the lot is in good order—last spring Mr. Wallis's stone fell over in a storm—and I could take these flowers."

At this moment Miss Pendexter took a good look at the bouquets, and found that they were as nearly alike as careful hands

clearly, apparently
fairness, with no preference

could make them. Mrs. Bickford was **evidently** trying to reach absolute **impartiality**.

thick

"I thought if I tied them up this afternoon," she said as she wound the first bunch of flowers with a **stout** string, "I could put them in a bucket of water now and then I should have all my time in the morning. I'll have a good deal to do before I go. I always sweep the living room and front entry Wednesdays. I want to leave everything nice, since I'm going away for all day. So I meant to get the flowers out of the way this afternoon. But I won't pick the rose 'til morning; it will be opened up better then."

"The rose?" questioned Miss Pendexter. "Why, are you going to pick that, too?"

"Yes, I am. I never like to let them fade on the bush. But that's just what's troubling me," and she turned to give a long, **imploring** look at the friend who sat beside her. Miss Pendexter had moved her chair closer. "I don't seem to know which of them ought to have it," said Mrs. Bickford **despondently**. "I do so hate to make a choice between my three dear deceased husbands. They all had their good points, especially Mr. Bickford, and I respected 'em all. I think as much of one of them as I do of the others."

"I truly sympathize," responded Miss Pendexter. "It's such a hard decision."

Both of the women felt as if they were powerless before a great emergency.

"There's one thing—They're all in a better world now." Said a sentimental Miss Pendexter, "they can't feel about a little thing like a rose the same as we can."

"No, I suppose it is myself that wants to be just," answered Mrs. Bickford. "I feel **obligations** to my last husband when I look around and see how comfortable he left me. Poor Mr. Wallis, my second husband, had his great projects, and perhaps if he had lived longer he'd have made a fortune; but when he died he was **in debt**. I had to get along almost any way I could for the next few years. Life was disappointing with Mr. Wallis, but he meant well, and he used to be an **amiable** person to live with, until his temper got spoiled from making so many hopes and having them all turn out failures. He did turn heads though, and dressed very handsome when I first met him. I don't know if you ever knew Mr. Wallis in his **prime**?"

"He died the year I moved over here from North Denfield," said Miss Pendexter, in a tone of sympathy. "I just knew him by sight. I went to his funeral."

"He should have had a better chance than he did in this little town. You see, he had excellent ideas, but he never learned the machinist's trade, and there was something wrong with every **invention** he built. His ideas were good, though. One time Mr. Wallis began talking about his **notions** and inventions to a man that traveled for a firm in Lowell, and that man wouldn't hardly stop to eat, he was so interested, and he said that he'd look for a job for him up in Lowell. It all sounded so well that I was ready to move there myself. But he never heard a word from him, and the disappointment was one he never got over. Somebody told me once that a man by the same name of the one from Lowell had got some **patents** for the very things Mr. Wallis used to be working on; but it was after he died, and I don't know if he ever could have really set

asking for help

very sadly

duties, promises

owing money

friendly

best part of life

new device

new ideas

government license to produce and sell a new product

things up so other folks could have seen their value. His machines used to break down more often than not.

"Then there was one day that spring," Mrs. Bickford sighed sentimentally, "when I couldn't find my **butter churn**, so I had to go and borrow one from the neighbors. I was so embarrassed, and it turns out he had taken ours all to pieces to get the parts to make some other useless appliance he'd invented. He had no business sense, but he was well meaning, and full of interesting conversation. I see now that he never had a fair chance to succeed. I've always felt bad about Mr. Wallis," said the old widow who was now Mrs. Bickford.

farm device to make butter from cream

"I'm sure you always speak well of him," said Miss Pendexter. "It was a pity he had never got among good business men, who could push his inventions and do all the business part."

"I was left very poor and needy for the next few years," said Mrs. Bickford sadly, "but he never gave up his dream that he would die a successful man. I don't see how I ever got along those next few years without him, but I did. I always **managed** to keep a pig, and sister Eliza gave me my potatoes, and I made out somehow.

was able

"Yes'm, you have everything to be thankful for," said Miss Pendexter, who was as poor herself at that moment as her friend had ever been. "Mr. Bickford was a very kind man," she quickly added, hoping to hear more **intimate** details of her old friend's past life.

private

"Oh, very kind," replied Mrs. Bickford, "There was something about him that was very **distinguished**. Strangers would always ask who he was as he walked into church. His words counted; he never spoke except when he had to. It was a relief at first after Mr. Wallis who was so **talkative**. But Mr. Wallis was **splendid** company for winter evenings. It would be bedtime before you knew it. I didn't used to listen to it all, but he had a great deal of information. Mr. Bickford, on the other hand, was very quiet. He didn't have the mind of my other husbands, but he was a very **dignified** appearing man. I remember that he used to almost always sleep in the evenings."

well-mannered and respected

always talking / wonderful

proud, high-class

"Those are lovely bouquets!" exclaimed Miss Pendexter. "Why, I couldn't tell them apart. The flowers are coming out just right aren't they?"

Mrs. Bickford nodded, and then suddenly remembering, she looked quickly at the rose in the window. In which bouquet should she put it?

"I always seem to forget about your first husband, Mr. Fraley," Miss Pendexter suggested bravely. "I've often heard you speak of him, too, but he'd passed away long before I ever knew you."

"He was just a boy," said Mrs. Bickford. "I thought the world was done for me when he died. Folks said we were as pretty a couple as ever came into church. We were both dark, with brown eyes and a good deal of color—I looked a lot better then than I do now! Albert held up his head, and looked as if he wanted to own the town, and he had a good word for everybody. I don't know what the years might have brought if he hadn't died so young."

The two old ladies were silent for a long time as Mrs. Bickford continued to **sort** the flowers into three bouquets.

separate

"I guess it was what they call falling in love," she added, in a different tone. "He was just a boy, and I was just a girl, but we were awfully happy. He was a strong, healthy young man who all of a sudden got a high fever and just died with no warning. We had just settled on a little farm, and he'd have done well if he'd had time. As it was, he left debts. But Albert had a lovely voice to sing. I could hear him singing to himself right out in the field **plowing or hoeing**. I didn't value it much at the time, but now when I think back, nothing ever sounded so sweet to me as the sound of his voice on that farm."

farm work to prepare ground for planting

Mrs. Bickford's own voice **trembled** a little, but she held up the last bouquet and examined it **critically**. "I must hurry now and put these in water," she said in a serious tone.

shook

judging carefully

"Yes, they do seem to **droop** a little," answered a sympathetic Miss Pendexter. "But you'll find they'll look very handsome tomorrow if you give them enough water. Folks will notice them from the road as they ride by the graveyard."

fall over, slouch

"They do look pretty, don't they?" Mrs. Bickford looked at all three bouquets. Then, turning to the lone red rose in the window, she **frowned**. "It seems foolish, but I'm still at a loss about that rose."

made a sad expression with the face

"I wish I had three roses, one for each husband," said Mrs. Bickford.

"Perhaps you'll feel sure when you first wake up in the morning," answered Miss Pendexter sympathetically. "I don't feel qualified to offer you any advice. I never was married myself, Mrs. Bickford."

"Well, I was married three times. I did the best I could while they were alive," the widow said, "and **mourned** them when I lost them, and I feel grateful to be left so comfortable now when all of it is over. I'm just a foolish old lady to worry so much about that rose."

observed a period of sadness

"And we both must be foolish old ladies to have been talking so long, wasting away this beautiful afternoon," said Misss Pendexter,

dead and still beloved

getting up to leave. "Please do enjoy your visit tomorrow, both with your sister's family and with your **dearly departed** late husbands."

II

The next morning, as she rode with her nephew away from her house, the widow had lost all spirit for her holiday. Perhaps it was the unusual excitement of the afternoon remembering her past life, or it might have been simply the bright moonlit night which had kept her awake until dawn, thinking of the past, and more concerned about the rose. By this time it had ceased to be merely a flower and had become a definite symbol and assertion of personal choice. She found it very difficult to decide on which grave it should be placed. So much of her present comfort and well-being was due to Mr. Bickford. Still, it was Mr. Wallis who had been the most unfortunate, and to whom she had done the least justice. If she

apologies or debts

owed recognition to Mr. Bickford, she certainly owed **amends** to Mr. Wallis. If she gave him the rose, it would be an affectionate apology. And then there was Albert, to whom she had no thought of

owing something

being either **indebted** or forgiving, but loved as if she were a young bride still. She could not escape from the terrible feeling of indecision.

It was after ten when she started her journey with the three large bouquets, covered with a newspaper to protect them from the sun. Even then she had not made up her mind. She had stopped trying to make a decision, and leaned back and rested as best she could.

"What an old fool I am," she said to herself in a loud whisper—too loud, because her nephew heard her.

"What ma'am?" he asked respectfully. But she did not answer. He was a handsome young man, but Mrs. Bickford still thought of him as a boy. He had always been her favorite among the younger members of the family. As they drove along, the widow suffering

great pain

the **acute agony** of indecision, the companionship of her nephew John grew every moment to be more and more a comfort. Sitting by his side, he was manly and cheerful, and she began to feel protected.

"Aunt Bickford" he suddenly announced, "I may as well say it now. I've got a piece of news to tell you, if you won't let it out to nobody. I guess you'll laugh, but you know I've always had something for Mary Lizzie Gifford ever since I was a boy. Well, we've got engaged."

"Well sir!" exclaimed Aunt Bickford with great interest. "I am
really pleased. She'll make you a good smart wife, John. Aren't all
the folks pleased, both sides?"

"Yes, they are," answered John with a happy, important look.

"I guess I can do something for you two to help along, when
the right time comes," said Aunt Bickford after a moment's reflection. "I've known what it is like to be starting out in life with plenty
of hope. When are you planning on getting married?"

"Early in the fall," said John **regretfully**. "I wish we could set
up housekeeping for ourselves right away this summer. I don't have
much, but I can work as well as anybody, and now is my time to
settle down."

"She's a nice, **modest**, pretty girl. I thought she liked you,
John," said the old aunt. "I saw her over at your mother's the last
day I was there. Well, I'm sure you'll be happy."

"Thank you, aunt," he said simply. "You're a real good friend to
me. She's coming over to spend the day with the girls," he added.
"Mother thought of it. You don't get over to see us very often."

Mrs. Bickford smiled happily. John's mother looked for her ap-
proval, no doubt, but it was very **proper** for John to have told her
the news himself, and in such a pretty way.

"My god!" said John suddenly. "I almost drove right by the
burying-ground. I forgot we wanted to stop."

Strange as it seemed, Mrs. Bickford herself had not noticed the
burying-ground, either, in her excitement and pleasure. But now she
felt **distressed** and responsible again, and it showed in her face at
once. The young man leaped to the ground, and reached for the
flowers.

"Here, you just let me run up with them," he said kindly. "It's
hot in the sun today. We'll stop tonight when I take you back, and
you can go up comfortably and visit the graves after sundown
when it's cool, and stay as long as you like. You seem sort of tired,
aunt."

"We'll maybe that's not a bad idea after all," said Mrs. Bickford
slowly.

To leave the matter of the rose in the hands of fate seemed
weak and **cowardly**, but there was not a moment for considera-
tion, and John was smiling, hands outstretched, and his suggestion
was a great relief. She watched him walk away, carrying the flowers
carefully, with a terrible **inward** shaking, and with sinking pride.
She felt weak and **numb**, and she leaned back and shut her eyes,
afraid she might shout instructions to her nephew which she might

sadly

not proud

socially correct

sad, anxious

without courage, afraid

inside the body
without feeling

regret. When finally she heard John running back along the path, she gave a sigh of relief. "I don't know why I had to go and pick that old rose anyway."

"I swear, they did look real handsome, aunt," said John's strong voice as he returned. "I set them up just as you told me. This one fell out, and I kept it. I hope you don't care. I can give it to Lizzie."

He faced her now with a happy, boyish look. There was something bright in his buttonhole—it was the red rose.

became red in the face

Aunt Bickford **blushed** like a girl. "Your choice is easily made," she said mysteriously, and then burst out laughing, right in front of the graveyard. "Come on, get in, dear," she said. "Well, well! I guess that rose was made for you. It looks very pretty in your coat, John."

She thought of Albert, and the next moment the tears came into her old eyes. John was a lover, too.

"My first husband was just such a tall, straight young man as you are," she said sentimentally as they drove along. "The flower he first gave me was a rose."

Reading Comprehension

1. Mrs. Bickford lived alone because
   a. she had never married.
   b. she was a widow.
   c. she was divorced.
2. Miss Pendexter came to Mrs. Bickford's house to visit because
   a. she was her neighbor.
   b. she wanted to walk to the graveyard with her.
   c. she admired the beautiful rose in her garden.
3. Mrs. Bickford was making three bouquets of flowers for
   a. her three sisters.
   b. her three friends.
   c. her three dead husbands.
4. Mrs. Bickford's first husband was
   a. an unsuccessful businessman.
   b. a farmer.
   c. a singer.
5. Mrs. Bickford's lived in a nice big house because
   a. Albert built a home for her.
   b. her family were successful farmers in Fairfield.
   c. her last husband was a wealthy man.

6. Her second husband never made any money because
   a. he never invented anything of value.
   b. he was a smart inventor, but a poor businessman.
   c. he died too young.
7. The widow was glad to let John put the flowers on her husbands' graves because
   a. she was too old to walk in the hot sun.
   b. she could not decide where to put the bouquet with the rose.
   c. he was her favorite nephew.
8. Of the three husbands she had married
   a. Albert was the love of her life, Mr. Wallis was the most boring, and her last husband left her with a comfortable inheritance.
   b. She loved her first husband the most, but tried to treat all three equally.
   c. Mr. Wallis was the only one who made a lot of money.

Vocabulary Check

Choose the sentence below that is closest in meaning to the model.

1. Mrs. Bickford usually sat by the window in the kitchen, unless she was solemnly stepping about doing her solitary housekeeping.
   a. Mrs. Bickford was, sadly, usually alone in her home.
   b. Mrs. Bickford lived a quiet life by herself, cooking, cleaning, and passing the day sitting by the kitchen window.
   c. Mrs. Bickford liked to sit by the kitchen window watching the flowers grow and waiting for a visitor.
2. The bright flower was like a face. Somehow, the beauty and life of it were surprising in the plain room, like a happy little child who might suddenly appear in a doorway.
   a. The beauty of the rose surprised and delighted the two old ladies so much that they acted as if they had just seen a happy little child.
   b. The rose looked like the face of a happy little child.
   c. While the ladies were looking at the rose, a small child appeared in the doorway.
3. The bouquets were as nearly alike as careful hands could make them. Mrs. Bickford was evidently trying to reach absolute impartiality.
   a. In honor of her three dead husbands, Mrs. Bickford had promised never to marry again.
   b. Mrs. Bickford was trying to hide the fact that she loved her first husband more than the other two.
   c. Mrs. Bickford carefully arranged the bouquets so that they looked exactly the same because she could not do anything that would appear to favor one husband over the others.

4. Miss Pendexter was as poor herself at that moment as her friend had ever been.
   a. While Mrs. Bickford had become rich after her third husband died, her friend Miss Pendexter was still very poor.
   b. Miss Pendexter, because she was getting old, was feeling poorly.
   c. Miss Pendexter, having never married, was a poor old lady.
5. "I'm still at a loss about that rose," said Mrs. Bickford.
   a. "I can't decide what to do with that rose."
   b. "I still haven't found that rose."
   c. "I couldn't sleep last night because I was thinking about that rose."
6. By this time it had ceased to be merely a flower and had become a definite symbol and assertion of personal choice.
   a. The rose began to wilt before Mrs. Bickford could decide on which grave to put it.
   b. The rose was not just a flower to Mrs. Bickford.
   c. To Mrs. Bickford, the rose was a sign that would point to the husband she loved best.
7. John told his aunt, "I've always had something for Mary Lizzie Gifford ever since I was a boy."
   a. "I've been in love with Mary Lizzie Gifford since I was a boy."
   b. "I've always had a ring to give Mary Lizzie Gifford ever since I was a boy."
   c. "Mary Lizzie Gifford was my first girlfriend."
8. "I wish we could set up housekeeping for ourselves right away this summer," said Johnny.
   a. "I wish we could live together as soon as this summer."
   b. "I wish we had enough money to get a housekeeper."
   c. "I wish we could keep the house for ourselves this summer."

Story Summary

1. On the line next to their names, copy the words that best describe each of Mrs. Bickford's three husbands.

first husband	poor	handsome	good singer
second husband	unlucky	dignified	good businessman
third husband	talkative	wealthy	farmer
youngest	boring	healthy	favorite
oldest	intelligent	inventor	

Albert Fraley ————————————————————————

————————————————————————————

Mr. Wallis ——————————————————————————

————————————————————————————

Mr. Bickford ————————————————————————

————————————————————————————

2. Now write three paragraphs, one about each dead husband. Write the name of each of Mrs. Bickford's husbands as the subject of the topic sentence of each paragraph. To describe each man, use the vocabulary you have written on p. 86.

Analyzing the Text

Although Mrs. Bickford's three late husbands had died many years before the story takes place, "The Only Rose" tells us a great deal about the lives of the three men. How does the reader get this information? Quickly reread the story, scanning each paragraph, looking for conversations between the two women in which Mrs. Bickford describes her husbands. When you find a paragraph about one of her husbands, in the right-hand margin write the name of the man that is the subject of the widow's conversation. You will then be able to go back to the story and easily locate the information you need to complete the following story summary exercise.

For example: The widow describes her husbands as follows:

"Oh, very kind," replied Mrs. Bickford, "There was something about him that was very distinguished. Strangers would always ask who he was as he walked into church. His words counted; he never spoke except when he had to. It was a relief at first after Mr. Wallis who was so talkative. But Mr. Wallis was splendid company for winter evenings. It would be bedtime before you knew it. I didn't used to listen to it all, but he had a great deal of information. Mr. Bickford, on the other hand, was very quiet. He didn't have the mind of my other husbands, but he was a very dignified appearing man. I remember that he used to almost always sleep in the evenings."

Interpreting Maps

Look at the map of the United States on page 77 in this chapter. It shows the dates when women were first allowed the same voting rights as men in each state. The names of many states are abbreviated. What are the full names of these states?

Study the map to find the information you need to answer the following questions:

1. What was the first state to allow women to vote?
2. What area of the country was first to approve women's suffrage?

3. What part of the United States was most opposed to women voting?
4. What was the only state on the East Coast to recognize women's rights before 1920?
5. Why aren't Alaska and Hawaii included in this map?

Grammar and Sentence Writing

The Present Perfect Continuous Tense

The present perfect continuous tense is a combination of the *present perfect tense,* which describes a past action from the point of view of the present time, and the *present continuous tense,* which describes an action taking place at the time of the conversation. It is formed by using "have been" or "has been" plus the present participle form of the main verb.

> **"I <u>have been hoping</u> that you would come to visit me today, Miss Pendexter."**

> The lonely widow <u>hoped</u> that her neighbor would visit her when she awoke in the morning, and she <u>is still hoping</u> that Miss Pendexter will visit today.

Combine the information in the two sentences below to form one sentence using the present perfect continuous tense.

Sentence Writing

MODEL:
Mrs. Bickford began living in her home when she married her third husband.
She is still living in the same home.

Mrs. Bickford has been living in the same home since she married her

third husband.

1. Mrs. Bickford began sitting at the kitchen table at breakfast.
   She is still sitting at the kitchen table.

   _____

   _____

   _____

2. The year began to go by quickly in January.
   Now in spring, the year is still passing quickly.

   _____

   _____

   _____

3. When her nephew left, Mrs. Bickford began to think about cleaning her house.
   She is still thinking about her housework.

   _____

   _____

   _____

4. When she became a widow, she began to visit her husbands' graves every spring.
   She still visits them every spring.

   _____

   _____

   _____

5. The flowers began to grow as soon as the weather became warmer.
   They are still growing now.

   _____

   _____

   _____

6. The widow wanted to go to the graveyard as soon as spring began.
   She still wants to visit her husbands' graves.

   _____

   _____

   _____

7. The old ladies began talking before noon.
   They are still talking, wasting a beautiful afternoon.

   _____

   _____

   _____

8. As soon as she saw the rose, she began to worry about what to do with it.
   She is still worrying about the rose at the graveyard.

   _____

   _____

9. Johnny and Lizzie began to think about getting married when they were still children.
   They still want to get married.

   _____

   _____

10. Mrs. Bickford began living alone when her third husband died.
    She still lives alone.

    _____

    _____

Writing About Yourself

Answer the following questions about yourself, using the present perfect continuous verb tense.

MODEL:
I have been doing my homework all morning.

1. How long have you been reading this book?

   _____

   _____

2. How long have you been taking this course?

   _____

   _____

3. How long have you been studying English?

   _____

   _____

4. How long have you been going to school?

   _____

   _____

5. How long have you been writing these sentences?

_____

_____

_____

Verbs after *Wish*

A *wish* is unreal, a dream or a fantasy. When verbs describe unreal actions, verb forms change. In verb clauses after "wish," actions in the present or future time are described with the past tense:

> **"I wish we <u>could</u> set up housekeeping for ourselves right away this summer," said John regretfully.**

> **"I wish I <u>had</u> three roses, one for each husband," said Mrs. Bickford.**

When we wish for something unreal in the past, we use the past conditional form:

> **Mrs. Bickford wishes that her husband <u>had not died</u>.**

The present tense of the verb "be" after wish is always "were" in formal English, never "was."

> **"I wish I <u>were</u> you" said Miss Pendexter to Mrs. Bickford, looking with envy at the lovely home Mr. Bickford left her neighbor when he died.**

Sentence Writing

Read the following sentences, then write your own sentences with "wish" or "wishes" to describe what the characters want, but what cannot be real. Begin each sentence with "she wishes."

MODEL:
Mrs. Bickford wants to have enough roses for each bouquet.
She wishes she had enough roses for each bouquet.

1. Miss Pendexter would like to have a big house like Mrs. Bickford's home.

_____

_____

_____

2. Mrs. Bickford wanted to spend her whole life with her first husband, Albert.

   _____

   _____

3. She regrets that Albert died so young.

   _____

   _____

4. "Mr. Wallis never met good businessmen who could sell his inventions," said Miss Pendexter.

   _____

   _____

5. Mrs. Bickford is upset because she does not know where to put the rose.

   _____

   _____

6. The two ladies are sad because they are very old.

   _____

   _____

7. Miss Pendexter was never married, so she cannot understand how her friend feels.

   _____

   _____

8. The widow does not like to live alone.

   _____

   _____

9. Albert is not alive, but Mrs. Bickford would love to still be with him.

   _____

   _____

10. The young couple cannot live together until they are married.

   _____

   _____

   _____

Word Forms

Choose the correct word to complete each sentence below.

sentiment   sentimental   sentimentally   sentiments

1. Thinking about her first husband always gave Mrs. Bickford

   _____ feelings.

2. Mrs. Bickford answered with unusual emotion. She normally did not

   speak with so much _____.

3. My first husband was just such a tall, straight young man as you are,"

   she said _____ as they drove along.

4. The two old ladies realized that the dead husbands could not share the

   same _____ about a rose as they did.

sympathetically   sympathetic   sympathy   sympathize

1. "I just knew him by sight. I went to his funeral," said Miss Pendexter, in

   a tone of _____.

2. "Yes, those flowers do seem to droop a little," answered a

   _____ Miss Pendexter.

3. "Perhaps you'll feel sure when you first wake up in the morning,"

   answered Miss Pendexter _____.

4. "I truly _____," responded Miss Pendexter. "It's such a hard

   decision."

decision   decide   undecided   decided   indecision

1. She found it very difficult to _____ on which grave the rose

   should be placed.

2. When she awoke the next morning, she still had not _____

   which husband should get the rose in his bouquet.

3. She could not escape from the terrible feeling of _____.

4. When she arrived at the graveyard, she was still _____.

5. She had stopped trying to make a _____, and leaned back and rested as best she could.

succeed   success   successful   unsuccessful

1. Her second husband never gave up his dream that he would become a _____ inventor.

2. Because he lived in a small town and did not know any good business-men, Mr. Wallis never had a fair chance to _____ in making money from his inventions.

3. Mr. Wallis died an _____ man, leaving the widow very poor and needy for the next few years.

4. Mr. Bickford, the widow's last husband, was older and less interesting than the others, but he had experienced financial _____ in his life.

Writing Comparative Sentences

Write sentences using comparatives as shown in the following models.

MODELS:
Mrs. Bickford was richer than Miss Pendexter.
The rose was more beautiful than the other flowers.
Mrs. Bickford was as old as Miss Pendexter.
Johnny was a better driver than Mrs. Bickford.

1. The two old ladies / sentimental / the three dead husbands

_____

_____

2. Mr. Bickford / talkative / Mr. Wallis

_____

_____

3. Albert / singer / Mr. Bickford

_____

_____

4. Mr. Bickford / businessman / Mr. Wallis

_____

_____

5. Mr. Bickford / rich / Mr. Wallis

_____

_____

6. Mr. Wallis / intelligent / Mr. Bickford

_____

_____

7. Her first marriage / happy / the other marriages

_____

_____

8. Albert / dignified and distinguished / Mr. Bickford

_____

_____

9. Mr. Bickford / quiet / Mr. Wallis

_____

_____

10. Miss Pendexter / poor / Mrs. Bickford had ever been

_____

_____

11. Her nephew John / tall and handsome / Albert, her first husband

_____

_____

12. Each bouquet / beautiful / the other bouquet

_____

_____

_____

Developing Ideas

Paragraph Writing

The perfect husband   1. Mrs. Bickford's three husbands were very different from each other. Like everyone, each man had his good points and his bad points. Read the way the widow describes her three dead husbands, and then combine the good characteristics of each to form one ideal, perfect husband who the widow might have married. Begin your paragraph with the phrase "Mrs. Bickford's perfect husband would . . ."

Remembering the dead   2. While Mrs. Bickford is worrying about her three dead husbands, Miss Pendexter reminds her old friend that: "They're all in a better world now. They can't feel about a little thing like a rose the same as we can." Do you think the dead are concerned about how we remember them? Is it important to keep alive the memory of our deceased family members, or is Miss Pendexter correct when she suggests that the dead do not care what the living do on this earth?

Mrs. Bickford's wishes   3. The widow has a comfortable life, but is she happy? Does she miss her husbands? Is she lonely? Is old age difficult for her? Do you think she raised any children during her three marriages? How do you think she would change her life if she could? Begin your paragraph with the phrase: "Mrs. Bickford wishes that . . ."

Topics for Discussion

1. The elderly in our society:
A *widow* is a woman whose husband has died but has not remarried. Mrs. Bickford is a widow, but she seems to never have had any children, so she is alone like her friend Miss Pendexter, who never married when she was younger. Are the elderly taken good care of in American society? Do you think Mrs. Bickford should live alone at her age, or should she be living with her sister and her family? Discuss how old people are taken care of in other societies. In other parts of the world are grandparents, great aunts and uncles, and other lonely old people treated differently than they are in the United States?

2. Why do men die younger than women?
There are far more lonely old widows in America than there are lonely old *widowers*—men whose wives have died. It is a fact that, on average, women can expect to live longer than men. Why do you think this is true?

Are men's lives more difficult? Do women take better care of their health? Are there biological differences between men and women that cause this difference in *longevity,* or length of a person's life? If possible, discuss this question in a mixed group of both male and female students.

3. The role of women in traditional New England society
After reading "The Only Rose," we know much more about Mrs. Bickford's three husbands than we do about the main character of the story. Why does she talk more about her late husbands than about herself? She seems to have lived her long life mainly as a companion to each of her three husbands. Sarah Orne Jewett felt strongly that women deserved equal rights and should enjoy individual freedom in American society, but at the time she wrote this story, females like the author were in fact second-class citizens. How have women's roles changed in modern times? Think of examples of women today who are as famous and powerful as their husbands, or maybe more so. Did such independent women also live at the time of "The Only Rose"?

For Further Discussion: Symbols

A symbol is an object or an act that means more than itself. Traditional symbols, like flowers, are easy to recognize. When you give someone flowers you are really giving a symbol of your love or respect. The rose in the title of this story represents something far more important than the plant Mrs. Bickford grew in her garden. Her problem deciding what to do with it symbolizes the conflict she feels when she compares her three late husbands. At the end of this story, when the rose is passed to a younger generation of lovers, the reader feels satisfied. The story has a happy ending. What does the ending of the story symbolize? What does it tell the reader about the old widow? What does this act tell us about the author's ideas of love and marriage?

The Bride Comes to Yellow Sky

STEPHEN CRANE

THE AUTHOR

Born in 1871, Stephen Crane died of tuberculosis in 1900, before reaching his twenty-ninth birthday. He devoted his short life to writing fiction. Although he was born after the Civil War had ended, his short novel The Red Badge of Courage *described the horrible bloodshed of that conflict so realistically that Crane quickly became famous after its publication in 1895. He then left the East to tour Texas and Mexico by railroad, where he visited fading cowboy towns like "Yellow Sky."*

THE STORY

Because life on the frontier was dangerous and uncomfortable, when Americans moved West they often left their wives and families behind. But the new railroads changed everything. Traveling was faster and more comfortable, and new products manufactured in the East could be transported to Western towns, making life easier. Now it was possible for men to bring wives to the small towns they had built. But cowboys were not used to their company. There were few women on the frontier, and they were treated with great respect.

In "The Bride Comes to Yellow Sky," Crane examines what happens when an old gunfighter marries and brings his bride out West.

Any woman moving West could expect surprises, but the bride in "Yellow Sky" must have been truly shocked to get off the train and immediately meet a drunken cowboy threatening to shoot her husband. But the gunman seemed equally shocked. Why would an armed cowboy be afraid of a defenseless woman?

I

The great passenger train was moving fast and smoothly over the plains of Texas, **heading** west, back to Yellow Sky, carrying Sheriff Potter and his new bride back home. The newly married couple in the **luxurious** Pullman coach had boarded the train at San Antonio. The man's face was red from many days in the wind and sun. Because he was used to wearing jeans and a cotton shirt, his stiff new black suit made him uncomfortable. He sat with a hand on each

going, pointing

full of luxury, elegant

The Cowboy Legend: The famous rough-living, horse-riding, pistol-carrying cowboy actually only existed for about twenty years following the American Civil War. In fact, many cowboys were ex-soldiers and former slaves. They found work herding cattle from pastures on the Great Plains to towns at the end of new railroad lines. Once the cowboys got their cows to the railroad, the cattle could be shipped back East to feed the growing population of America's cities. But the railroads soon stretched all the way across the country, farmers built fences on the prairie and converted the land to private property, and the cowboy era came to an end.

quick looks
secret

knee, nervously. The **glances** he gave other passengers were **furtive** and shy.

The sheriff's bride sat next to him. Despite the fancy dress that she wore, she was not very pretty. She appeared to be about thirty years old, of a working-class background. Now that she had married, she could look forward to many years of cooking and cleaning for her new husband.

a recently married
couple

not belonging, not
fitting in

Neither of the **newlyweds** was accustomed to such luxurious travel, so they were very happy, even though many of the other passengers were staring and grinning at the obviously **out-of-place** couple.

Railroads of the Old West

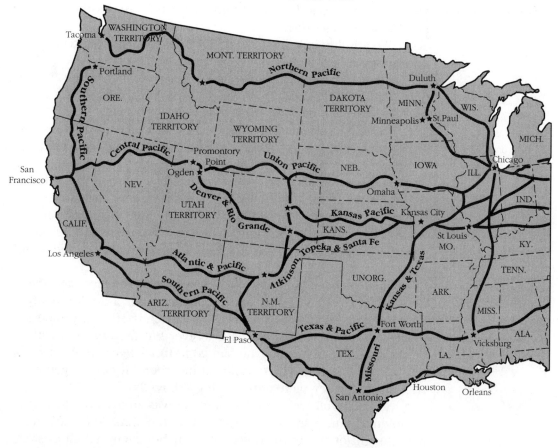

By 1884 railroads connected the Wild West to the eastern United States. The hero of this story meets his bride in San Antonio, and they ride the train to the fictional town of Yellow Sky, located somewhere in western Texas near El Paso.

"Ever been on a train before?" he asked her, smiling with delight.

"No," she answered; "I never was. It's fine, **ain't** it?"

"It's great! After a while we'll go forward to the dining car and get a big feed. They charge a whole dollar, because it's the finest meal in the world."

"Oh, do they?" cried the bride. "Charge a dollar? Why, that's too much for us, ain't it, Jack?"

"Not this trip, anyhow," he answered bravely. "We're going to go the whole way."

Later he explained to her about the trains. "You see, it's a thousand miles from one end of Texas to the other; and this train runs

(nonstandard) isn't

right across it, and never stops but four times." Because Potter had traveled on the train before, it made him proud to **display** this knowledge to his bride.

show or demonstrate

"We are due in Yellow Sky at 3:42," he said, looking tenderly into her eyes.

At last they went to the dining car, and ate a grand meal. Then they returned to the coach to watch the endless miles of Texas roll by.

But as the distance from Yellow Sky grew shorter, the husband grew more **restless**. As a matter of fact, Jack Potter was beginning to get very nervous. He, the sheriff of Yellow Sky, a man known, liked, and feared, a well-respected person, had gone to San Antonio to meet a girl he believed he loved, and there, after the usual prayers, had actually married her, without telling anyone in Yellow Sky. Because he knew everyone in the community would be surprised and **shocked**, he was not **looking forward** to bringing his bride back home.

uneasy, unable to rest

horrified, disgusted / eagerly awaiting

Of course, people in Yellow Sky were free to marry, and the town often celebrated their marriages, but Potter, a **bachelor** of long standing, thought of his duty to his friends. He had promised them he would remain a bachelor forever, but **face to face** with this woman in San Antonio, he had gone **head over heels**. Because no one knew him in San Antonio, he had found it easy to get married. But now they were approaching Yellow Sky.

an unmarried man

in the presence of

(had done something) hastily, rashly

He knew full well that his marriage was an important thing in his town. The men in town would not forgive him. Frequently he had thought of telling them by telegraph, but even though as sheriff he had often faced the guns of **outlaws** without fear, he was afraid to do it. And now the train was hurrying him toward his friends, who would laugh at him, **curse** him, and never drink with him again.

criminals

swear at

Knowing that soon the train would leave them standing by the tracks in Yellow Sky, he planned the trip from the station to his house. They would get to his home as fast as possible, so no one would see them. Then, once home, he would quietly go out alone, tell someone—anyone—the awful news, and **retreat** to his house to hide until the citizens got tired of talking about him and his new bride.

move back from danger

The bride looked **anxiously** at him. "What's worrying you, Jack?" Her voice reminded him that he was still on the train, so he laughed. "I'm not worryin', girl; I'm only thinkin' of Yellow Sky."

nervously, with worry

She **blushed** in comprehension.

became red in the face from embarrassment

The porter came and told the sheriff the train was nearing Yellow Sky. He brushed his new clothes, and then helped the bride get her suitcase from under the seat. Because he had seen others do it, the old cowboy **fumbled** out a coin to give the porter. The newlyweds were now ready to meet the town.

handled clumsily, groped

II

Meanwhile, as the train neared town, six men stood at the bar of the Yellow Sky **Saloon**. One was a traveling salesman who talked a great deal and rapidly; three were Texans who did not care to talk at that time because they were **concentrating** on a **poker** game; and two were **sheepherders** who never talked when they were in the Yellow Sky Saloon. An old dog lay sleeping on the board sidewalk outside the saloon's door. The sandy main street, baking in the midday sun, was empty. Except for the men in the saloon, Yellow Sky was **dozing**.

tavern in the Old West

thinking intensely about / a card game / persons who tend sheep

sleeping lightly

The traveling salesman was telling a story when he was interrupted by a young man who suddenly appeared in the open door. He cried: "Scratchy Wilson is drunk, and he's shooting up the town!" The shepherds at once set down their glasses and ran out the rear door.

The friendly salesman answered the newcomer at the door: "All right, my friend, so what? Come in and have a drink."

The young man only **frowned**. The room had suddenly become very quiet. Because the warning had made such an **obvious** impression on everyone, even the salesman became worried.

looked with displeasure / apparent, immediately evident

"Say, what is this?" he asked.

"It means, my friend," the newcomer answered, as he came into the saloon, "that for the next two hours this town won't be a healthy place."

The **barkeeper** went to the door and locked it; reaching out the window, he pulled in the heavy wooden **shutters** and **barred** them.

person in charge of the bar, who serves drinks / movable window coverings / closed or locked with a heavy stick of wood

"But say," the salesman cried, "what is this, anyhow? You don't mean there is going to be a gunfight?"

"I don't know whether there'll be a fight or not," answered one man **grimly**; "but there'll be some shootin'—some good shootin'!"

seriously, sternly

The young man who had warned them waved his hand. "Oh, there'll be a fight soon enough, if anyone wants it. Anybody can get a fight out there in the street. There's a fight just waiting."

"What did you say his name was?" the salesman asked.

"Scratchy Wilson," they answered **in chorus**.

as a group, all together

"And will he kill anybody? What are you going to do? Does this happen often? Does he do this once a week or so? Can he break in that door?"

"No, he can't break down that door," replied the barkeeper. "He's tried it three times. But when he comes you'd better lie down on the floor, because he's sure to shoot at the door, and a bullet may come through."

With one eye on the door, the salesman moved closer to the wall. "Will he kill anybody?" he asked.

The men laughed at the question.

"He's out to shoot, and he's out for trouble. He'll kill anybody that gets in his way."

"But what do you do in a case like this?"

A man responded: "Why, Jack Potter will take care of him—"

"But," the other men interrupted in chorus, "Jack Potter's in San Antonio."

"Well, who is he? What's he got to do with it?"

"Oh, he's the sheriff. He goes out and fights Scratchy when he gets wild."

"Wow!" said the salesman, **mopping his brow**. "Nice job he's got!"

wiping sweat from the forehead

The barkeeper took a Winchester rifle from beneath the bar. He looked at the worried salesman.

"You'd better come behind the bar with me."

"No, thanks," said the salesman, **perspiring**. "I'd rather be where I can run for the back door."

sweating

"You see," the barkeeper explained, "Scratchy Wilson is an expert with a gun; and when he goes on the warpath, we hide—naturally. He's about the last one of the old **gang** that used to hang out along the river here. He's a **terror** when he's drunk. When he's **sober** he's all right—kind of simple—wouldn't hurt a fly—the nicest fellow in town. But when he's drunk—he's a killer."

group of outlaws

something causing great fear / not drunk

There was a period of silence. Then the barkeeper said, "I wish Jack Potter was back from San Antonio. He shot Wilson once—in the leg—and he would **straighten him out** now."

correct his behavior

Then they heard from a distance the sound of a gunshot, followed by three wild yells. The men in the darkened saloon looked at each other. "Here he comes," they said.

III

Wilson was drunk. He stood in the middle of the main street, waving a long, heavy, blue-black **revolver** in each hand. He yelled loudly, and his cries **echoed** off the closed and locked houses of the village. He shot both guns into the air, yelling again, **challenging** anyone to fight him. But only the silence of the Western plains answered his war-cry, so he **staggered** down the street, heading for the Yellow Sky Saloon.

Wilson looked like a wild man. Because he had been drinking all day, his eyes rolled around in his head, his knees **buckled** as he walked, and his mouth spat out a steady stream of curses. As he walked down the middle of the street, he pointed his guns into each doorway, but because the people of the town were used to his **rampages**, no one came out to meet him.

There was no offer of fight. The man called to the sky. There was no answer. He yelled and screamed and pointed his revolvers here and everywhere.

Finally Wilson got to the closed front of the Yellow Sky Saloon. He went up to it and, hammering the door with a revolver, demanded drink.

The door would not open, so he walked back across the street, turned quickly, and fired six shots, all hitting within inches of the big brass doorknob that had **offended** him. He swore to himself and went away. Later, he went to the house of his best friend, who would not come outside, and casually shot out all his windows.

Still there was no one who dared to fight him. Then he remembered his **arch-enemy**, Jack Potter, and staggered off to his house. He was sure that if he shot at the sheriff's house, Potter would come out to fight him.

When he arrived at Potter's house, it was as quiet as the rest of the town. Standing behind a big oak tree, he fired a shot at the door.

"Come out and fight, Potter! I plan to pay you back for shootin' up my leg!" he yelled.

But the house was silent. No door opened; no sound was heard. Wilson went into a **rage**, cursing, yelling, and firing bullet after bullet into the windows. Because Potter was the sheriff, the drunken cowboy felt that Potter had a duty to fight him. He was **outraged** at the silence that answered his gunfire. Finally, because he had emptied both his guns, he was forced to stop shooting and take a rest. Cursing the absent sheriff, Wilson sat down in the shade of the tree to reload his revolvers.

---

a type of pistol

resounded, bounced back / demanding or calling for a fight or a contest

walked unsteadily, almost falling

bent uncontrollably

states of wild, violent behavior

insulted, made angry

worst enemy

violent fit of temper

offended, furious

IV

Meanwhile, as Wilson was resting under the tree in front of Potter's house, the express train had left the sheriff and his bride at the station. Relieved that there had been no one there to meet him, Potter led his wife down the street toward his small house.

"Next corner, dear," he said finally.

They walked together, hand in hand, looking forward to getting home at last. Potter was about to point to the new home when, as they turned the corner, they came face to face with a man who was pushing **cartridges** into a large revolver. Immediately the man dropped his revolver to the ground and, like lightning, **whipped** another from its **holster**. The second gun was **aimed** at the **bridegroom**'s chest.

There was a silence. Potter's mouth hung open. He quickly let go of his new wife's hand and dropped the suitcase he had been carrying. As for the bride, her face had turned yellow. She stood, frozen at his side, staring into the end of Wilson's gun.

The two men stood only six feet apart. Wilson, holding the gun on the sheriff, smiled with joy and confidence.

"Tried to **sneak up** on me," he said. "Tried to sneak up on me!" His eyes grew more serious. As Potter made a slight movement, the man stuck his revolver forward. "No; don't you do it, Jack Potter. Don't you move a finger toward a gun just yet. Don't you move an **eyelash**. The time has come for me to **settle** with you, and I'm goin' to do it my own way. I'm the boss now, so if you don't want a bullet in you, just do what I tell you."

Potter looked at his enemy. "I ain't got a gun on me, Scratchy," he said. "Honest, I ain't. You know I fight when it comes to fighting, Scratchy Wilson; but I ain't got a gun on me, so you'll have to do all the shooting yourself."

Wilson's face went red. He stepped forward and pushed his weapon into Potter's chest. "Don't you tell me you ain't got no gun on you, you skunk. Don't tell me no lie like that. There ain't a man in Texas ever seen you without no gun. Don't take me for a kid." His eyes burned with light, and his gun shook in his hand.

"I ain't sayin' you're a kid," answered Potter. His heels had not moved an inch backward. "I'm takin' you for a damn fool. I tell you I ain't got a gun, and I ain't. If you're going to shoot me, you'd better begin now; you'll never get another chance like this."

Because he was totally confused, Wilson didn't know what to do. He thought for a moment before asking, "If you ain't got a gun,

---

Margin glosses:

unfired shells or bullets

pulled suddenly / leather holder for a pistol, usually worn on a belt / pointed / newly married man

surprise by secretly moving close

one of the short, fine hairs around the eye / pay a debt, get even

why ain't you got a gun?" He laughed, "Have you been to **Sunday school**?"

"I ain't got a gun because I've just come from San Antonio with my wife. I'm married," said Potter. "And if I'd thought there was going to be any skunks like you running around when I brought my wife home, I'd have had a gun, and don't you forget it."

"Married!" said Scratchy, not at all understanding.

"Yes, married. I'm married," said Potter, clearly.

"Married?" said Scratchy. For the first time, he saw the frightened woman at the sheriff's side. "No!" It seemed **incredible** to Wilson that the sheriff would take a bride. He moved a foot backward, and his arm, with the revolver, dropped to his side. "Is this the lady?" he asked.

"Yes," answered Potter.

"Pleased to meet you," Wilson said shyly.

There was another period of silence.

"Well," said Wilson at last, slowly, "I suppose it's all off now. I can't kill a man standing next to his new bride. You coward, Potter! It ain't **fair**."

"It's all off if you say so, Scratchy. You know I didn't make the trouble." Potter picked up the suitcase.

"Well, I guess it's over, Jack," said Wilson. He was looking at the ground. "Married!" Because he was not used to the company of married ladies, he felt uncomfortable. "Uh, goodbye, **ma'am**," he **stammered**, now suddenly sober. He picked up his other revolver and placed both weapons in their holsters. He hung his head as he walked away, **shuffling** along the sandy street.

Margin glosses:
- religious school for children
- amazing, unbelievable
- proper under the rules
- short form of *madame,* a term of respect for women / stuttered, spoke haltingly / walking without lifting the feet

Reading Comprehension

1. Potter was afraid to tell his friends in Yellow Sky that he had married because
   a. he already had a wife.
   b. his bride was ugly.
   c. they had expected him to remain a bachelor forever.
2. The sheriff and his bride enjoyed the train ride because
   a. they had never been to Texas before.
   b. they were unaccustomed to such luxurious travel.
   c. they were looking forward to getting home to Yellow Sky.

3. The door of the Yellow Sky Saloon was closed and barred to Scratchy Wilson because
   a. he wouldn't pay his bar bill.
   b. he always insulted the ladies.
   c. he was drunk and shooting up the town.
4. Wilson was staggering through the streets of the town looking for
   a. anyone who would fight him.
   b. his horse.
   c. some friends to talk with.
5. When Wilson was sober, he
   a. robbed banks.
   b. was always looking for fights.
   c. was the nicest fellow in town.
6. Wilson was glad he ran into Potter in front of his house because
   a. Potter owed him money.
   b. he wanted to meet Potter's bride.
   c. he felt that the sheriff would surely fight him.
7. Potter was not carrying a gun because
   a. he had sold it in San Antonio.
   b. he had just come from San Antonio with his wife.
   c. he had quit his job as sheriff.
8. Wilson did not shoot Potter because
   a. he couldn't shoot an unarmed man standing next to his bride.
   b. he forgave him for shooting him in the leg.
   c. his gun was empty.

Vocabulary Check

Choose the sentence below that is the closest in meaning to the model.

1. The other passengers stared at the out-of-place couple.
   a. The other passengers stared at the couple that looked like they didn't belong there.
   b. The other passengers stared at the funny-looking couple.
   c. The other passengers stared at the well-dressed, handsome couple.
2. Potter was not looking forward to bringing his bride back home.
   a. Potter thought they would arrive home very late.
   b. Potter was afraid of what might happen when he brought his bride back home.
   c. Potter was sorry that he had gotten married.

3. Face to face with this woman in San Antonio, he had gone head over heels.
   a. When he saw the face of the woman in San Antonio, he turned on his heels and ran.
   b. When he saw the woman in San Antonio, he went a little wild and did something unusual.
   c. When he first saw the woman in San Antonio, he was so excited he fell down.
4. The salesman was mopping his brow.
   a. The salesman was cleaning the bar.
   b. The salesman was making a sad face.
   c. The salesman was wiping the sweat from his forehead.
5. Scratchy whipped his gun from its holster.
   a. Scratchy suddenly pulled out his gun from its holster.
   b. Scratchy shook out his gun from its holster.
   c. Scratchy threw out his gun from its holster.
6. "Tried to sneak up on me!" he said.
   a. "You tried to surprise me!" he said.
   b. "You tried to hide from me!" he said.
   c. "You tried to insult me!" he said.
7. The time has come for me to settle with you.
   a. It's too late for us to live together.
   b. I'm going to pay the debt I owe you right now.
   c. It's time for us to make a deal.
8. It seemed incredible to Wilson that the sheriff would take a bride.
   a. Wilson couldn't believe that the sheriff would take a bride.
   b. Wilson thought it was very funny that the sheriff had gotten married.
   c. Wilson thought that only a blind woman would marry the sheriff.

Story Summary

By answering the following questions, you will write a paragraph that summarizes the story.

What did Sheriff Potter acquire in San Antonio? Where was he bringing her? Describe the feeling of the newlyweds as they traveled across Texas. Why was Potter not looking forward to getting back home? Did anyone in Yellow Sky know he was coming, or who was with him? What was happening in Yellow Sky as the sheriff and his bride were nearing the town? Why was Scratchy Wilson shooting up the town? Why wouldn't anyone fight Wilson? Who usually fought him when he got drunk? Why did the drunken cowboy go to Potter's house? How did he feel when the sheriff didn't come out to fight? When he finally met the sheriff, why didn't

Wilson shoot Potter? How did he feel about the sheriff's marriage? What would have happened if Potter's bride hadn't been standing next to him when Wilson surprised him?

Analyzing the Text

Sheriff Potter: A Brave Cowboy?

Typically, the cowboy sheriff was known as a brave man, a hero not afraid of fighting outlaws or Indians. But Crane's story is humorous because the sheriff of Yellow Sky is afraid of one thing: the reactions of his friends when they find out that he has gotten married. This story of gunfighters and sheriffs shows the reader another side of cowboy life. While western men seemed fearless, they were uncomfortable in unfamiliar situations, and in the company of respectable ladies. Reread the story to discover Potter's reaction to the different situations he faces as the plot unfolds. In each case listed below, how does he feel?

In the spaces provided below, choose the adjective that best describes Sheriff Potter's feelings at the time:

afraid	uncomfortable	proud
ashamed	brave	happy

1. Potter gets married in San Antonio. _____

2. Potter dresses up in a new suit. _____

3. Potter rides the train with his new wife. _____

4. Potter explains to his new bride how the trains work. _____

5. Potter thinks about how he can tell his friends that he got married.

_____

6. Potter, unarmed himself, faces the pointed gun of Scratchy Wilson.

_____

Interpreting Maps

Railroads in the West

Look at the map of railroads in the western United States in 1884 on page 101. For the first time, the United States was connected, from East Coast to West Coast, by a reliable means of transportation.

1. There were far fewer people in this land during the days of the cowboys. Much of the west was still wild "territories." Which states were still wilderness in 1884? Compare this map with the map of the United States shown in the introduction to Chapter 4.
2. Many large cities of today's West and Great Plains began as outposts on the railroad. What modern cities were not on the map of 1884?
3. The names of the nineteenth century railroads appear above their lines on the map. Which of these railroad companies still exist today?
4. To reach Yellow Sky, the sheriff and his bride rode the train from San Antonio to western Texas. From what railroad company did they buy their ticket?

Grammar and Sentence Writing

Using *Because* and *So* to Combine Related Ideas

He was used to wearing jeans and a cotton shirt.
His new suit made him uncomfortable.

Because the two ideas expressed above are related, they can be combined into one sentence. We could use *and* to join the two simple sentences, but this would not help explain the nature of the relationship. The relationship between the two clauses, one of cause and effect, can be precisely stated with *because*.

Because he was used to wearing jeans and a cotton shirt, his new suit made him uncomfortable.

A simple clause beginning with *because* is not a complete sentence. It needs another clause explaining its effect.

Because he had been a bachelor for many years . . .

The clause above is not a complete sentence, but a fragment. When reading this, the reader might ask, "So what?"

The whole town was surprised when he got married.

The above independent clause is needed to make the complete sentence:

Because he had been a bachelor for many years, the whole town was surprised when he got married.

The *because* clause may be written following the independent clause. Note that no comma is now used:

The whole town was surprised when he got married because he had been a bachelor for many years.

For variety, *so* can be used in place of *because* when the independent clause follows:

He had been a bachelor for many years, so the whole town was surprised when he got married.

Sentence Combining

Combine the following sentences as shown in the models below.

MODEL:
His new suit made him uncomfortable. He was used to wearing jeans and a cotton shirt. (because)

Because he was used to wearing jeans and a cotton shirt, his new suit made him uncomfortable.

MODEL:
The newlyweds were not accustomed to such luxurious travel. They were very happy. (so)

The newlyweds were not accustomed to such luxurious travel, so they were very happy.

1. They charge a dollar. It is the finest meal in the world. (because)

   _____

   _____

2. Potter had traveled on the train before. It made him proud to display his knowledge to his bride. (so)

   _____

   _____

3. He was not looking forward to bringing his bride back home. He knew everyone would be shocked. (because)

   _____

   _____

4. No one knew him in San Antonio. It had been easy to get married. (because)

_____

_____

5. They would go to his home as fast as possible. No one would see them. (so)

_____

_____

6. His wife reminded him he was still on the train. He laughed. (so)

_____

_____

7. He had seen others do it. The old cowboy gave a coin to the porter. (because)

_____

_____

8. He had seen others do it. The old cowboy gave a coin to the porter. (so)

_____

_____

9. The Texans did not care to talk at that time. They were concentrating on a poker game. (because)

_____

_____

10. The Texans did not care to talk at that time. They were concentrating on a poker game. (so)

_____

_____

_____

11. The warning had made an obvious impression on everyone. Even the salesman became worried. (because)

_____

_____

12. The warning had made an obvious impression on everyone. Even the salesman became worried. (so)

_____

_____

13. Wilson is an expert with a gun. When he goes on the warpath, we hide. (so)

_____

_____

14. Wilson had been drinking all day. His eyes rolled around in his head. (because)

_____

_____

15. Potter was the sheriff. The drunken cowboy felt that Potter had a duty to fight him. (because)

_____

_____

16. Potter was the sheriff. The drunken cowboy felt that Potter had a duty to fight him. (so)

_____

_____

_____

Sentence Completion

Using the clauses below, add your own words to form complete sentences. Write *the entire sentence* in the space provided. Then write the same sentence again, but use *so* in place of *because* to join the two clauses.

MODEL:
The poker players weren't talking because . . .

The poker players weren't talking because they were concentrating on the

game.

(so)

The poker players were concentrating on the game, so they weren't talking.

1. Because the sheriff's friends were bachelors . . .

_____

_____

(so)

_____

_____

2. Scratchy didn't shoot the sheriff because . . .

_____

_____

(so)

_____

_____

3. The men in the saloon were afraid of Wilson because . . .

_____

_____

(so)

_____

_____

Sentence Writing

Writing complete sentences, answer these questions. Use *because* or *so* in each answer, and remember that each answer must have two clauses.

MODEL:
Why didn't Sheriff Potter tell anyone he had gotten married?

Potter didn't tell anyone because he thought they would laugh at him.

1. Why was the sheriff uncomfortable in his fancy new clothes?

_____

_____

2. Why were Potter and his bride riding the train?

_____

_____

3. Why did the barkeeper close the windows and lock the door to the saloon?

_____

_____

4. Why was Scratchy Wilson shooting up the town?

_____

_____

5. What had Potter done to make Wilson want to shoot him?

_____

_____

6. Why didn't Potter come out of his house when Wilson shot at the windows?

_____

_____

7. Why didn't Wilson shoot Potter when he had the chance?

_____

_____

_____

Changing Direct Quotations to Indirect Quotations

"Ever been on a train before?" he asked.
He asked if she had ever been on a train before.

The two sentences above state the same information, but they are written differently because the first sentence is a DIRECT QUOTATION, repeating the exact words spoken by the subject. Quotation marks (" ") enclose those words spoken by the subject.

When DIRECT QUOTATIONS are written, slang expressions and contractions not usually used in formal writing, but common in casual conversation, are often included:

"Why, that's too much for us, ain't it, Jack?"

The above sentence would be written quite differently as an INDI-RECT QUOTE:

She asked if that was not too much for them.

The apostrophe (') is used to show letters left out when forming contractions, and it also is used in direct quotes to show beginning or ending sounds of words that are omitted in speech:

"I'm worryin' 'cause I'm thinkin' of Yellow Sky," he said.

Written as an indirect quote, this sentence would be:

He said he was worrying because he was thinking of Yellow Sky.

Because direct quotes use the exact words spoken by the subject, verbs are often in the present or future tense, even though the story is told in the past tense:

"After a while we'll go to the dining car and get a big meal," he said.

When the sentence above is changed to an indirect quote, *we'll,* the contraction for *we will,* must be changed to "we would" to agree with the main verb *said,* which is in the past tense. Note that the pronouns are also changed to the third person.

He said that after a while they would go to the dining car and get a big meal.

Writing Indirect Quotations

Change the following direct quotations to indirect quotations as in the model below.

MODEL:
One man answered, "There'll be some shootin'—some good shootin'!"

One man answered that there would be some shooting—some good

shooting.

1. "Will he kill anybody?" he asked.
   He asked if _____

2. He said, "He's a terror when he's drunk, but when he's sober he wouldn't hurt a fly."

   _____

   _____

3. "Wilson is an expert with a gun, and when he goes on the warpath we hide—naturally," he whispered.

   He whispered that _____

   _____

4. "I wish Jack Potter was back from San Antonio," said the barkeeper.

   The barkeeper said _____

   _____

5. "I plan to pay you back for shootin' up my leg!" he yelled.

   He yelled that _____

   _____

6. "The time has come for me to settle with you, and I'm goin' to do it my own way," said Wilson.

   _____

   _____

   _____

7. "There ain't a man in Texas ever seen you without a gun," he said.

   _____

   _____

   _____

8. "I ain't got a gun because I've just come from San Antonio with my wife," Potter answered.

   _____

   _____

   _____

Using the Apostrophe to Show Possession

The apostrophe (') is used in place of missing letters in contractions and abbreviated words. In dialogue using direct quotations the apostrophe is frequently used this way:

"I can't shoot you when your wife's standin' next to you!" said Wilson.

But the apostrophe has another important function. It is used to show a close relationship between two nouns:

Wilson was surprised to meet the *wife* of the *sheriff*.

The above sentence can be more conveniently written:

Wilson was surprised to meet the *sheriff's wife*.

To form the possessive of most nouns, add *'s*. But when the noun already ends in *s*, just add the apostrophe at the end of the word.

The sheriff was staring at the *outlaw's* guns.
The sheriff was staring at the two *outlaws'* guns.

In the second sentence above, because there are two outlaws, the noun ends in *s*, so the apostrophe is placed after the word. In the first sentence the apostrophe separates the *s* from the noun *outlaw* to avoid confusing the plural with the singular form.

Now rewrite the sentences in the following exercise, using apostrophes to show possession where possible.

Forming Possessives

Use apostrophes to form possessives in each of the sentences below.

MODEL:
In the Old West it was the duty of the sheriff to carry a gun.

In the Old West it was the sheriff's duty to carry a gun.

MODEL:
The stiff new suit of the sheriff made him uncomfortable.

The sheriff's new suit made him uncomfortable.

1. The newlyweds enjoyed their meal in the luxurious dining car of the passenger train.

2. The new bride of the sheriff sat next to him.

3. As the train approached Yellow Sky, the new bride noticed the uneasiness of her husband.

4. Potter was afraid of the reaction of his bachelor friends to his marriage.

   _____

   _____

5. The sheriff gave the porter a tip for getting the suitcase of his bride from under the seat.

   _____

   _____

6. When they found out that he was drunk, everyone in town hid because of the reputation of Scratchy Wilson.

   _____

   _____

7. The bartender closed and locked the door and windows of the saloon.

   _____

   _____

8. Because he had been drinking all day, the eyes of Wilson rolled around in his head.

   _____

   _____

9. Wilson was embarrassed when he met the bride of the sheriff.

   _____

   _____

10. When Potter saw the gun of Scratchy Wilson, he dropped the suitcase of his wife.

    _____

    _____

Word Forms

Choose the correct word to complete each sentence below.

luxurious   luxury   luxuriously

1. The sheriff and his bride enjoyed dining on the train because they were

   not used to such _____ .

2. The newly married couple in the _____ Pullman coach had

boarded the train in San Antonio.

3. The dining car was _____ decorated.

comfort   comfortable   comfortably
uncomfortable   uncomfortably

1. Potter's bride made Scratchy feel _____ .

2. Potter's old cowboy clothes fit more _____ than the new shirt

and pants he wore on the train.

3. The passengers on the train rode across Texas in great_____ .

4. Many old cowboys like Scratchy Wilson did not feel _____ in

the company of ladies.

5. The sun in Yellow Sky at noon was _____ hot.

nervous   nervously   nervousness

1. It made Potter _____ to think of his arrival in Yellow Sky.

2. The men in the saloon _____ hid behind the bar.

3. The barkeeper could see the traveling salesman's _____ .

echo   echoed   echoing

1. Scratchy Wilson's yells _____ through the streets of Yellow Sky.

2. The only answer he heard was the _____ of his own voice.

3. The nervous men in the saloon heard the gunshots _____

through the street.

Developing Ideas

Guided Paragraph Writing

Sample Paragraph A   I'm Sheriff Potter's new bride. After we got married, I was looking forward to moving to Yellow Sky. I thought I would be happy living in a new town with a new husband to care for. Because the sheriff has an important job, I thought I would be treated with respect in Yellow Sky. But I didn't realize the problems I would have! The first person I met in my new town was a drunken cowboy who was pointing his guns at my husband and me! I thought I would never live long enough to enjoy my marriage, but fortunately he didn't shoot us.

Writing Assignment   After reading the above paragraph, write your own paragraph about a surprise you had when you first got married, moved to a new town, attended a new school, or began a new job. Tell what your feelings were before you were surprised, what happened that you did not expect, and how you reacted to this surprise.

Sample Paragraph B   My name is Sheriff Potter. After living as a bachelor for many years in Yellow Sky, I suddenly got married in San Antonio. Because I had often told my friends that I would never marry, I was too embarrassed to tell anyone back home that I had gotten married. I was afraid that everyone would laugh, so when we got off the train I hurried home with my bride, hoping that no one would see us together. But to my great surprise, my archenemy Scratchy Wilson was waiting in front of my house, drunk and ready for a fight. Just as he was going to shoot me, he realized that the frightened woman standing next to me was my new bride, so he didn't pull the trigger. He was more embarrassed than I was! Although I had been so embarrassed I couldn't tell anyone that I had a wife, she actually saved my life!

Writing Assignment   After reading Sample Paragraph B, write your own paragraph about something you did that you were too embarrassed to talk about. How did everyone find out? What was their reaction? Was it as bad as you thought it would be?

Topics for Discussion

Form a small group with some of your classmates and discuss the following topics:

1. The Cowboy Legend

The American cowboy is known all over the world, yet he only rode the West for a few years late in the nineteenth century. Why have so many stories, movies, and television shows been made about cowboys? Do other countries have heroes from their history that are still popular today? (Consider the samurai of Japan, or England's pirates.) Why are cowboy stories, and other stories of legendary heroes, filled with violence? Is this why they are so popular, or are there other reasons?

2. Women in the Old West

The typical hero of a Western story is not married. The frontier was considered a man's world, but how could any society exist without women? Why aren't there more women with important roles in cowboy tales? In "The Bride Comes to Yellow Sky," what kind of life could Potter's wife look forward to? Would many women today want a marriage like hers? Was life for men more comfortable, or did both men and women work hard? Did men have more privileges than women? Did women enjoy special privileges too? (Would Scratchy Wilson shoot a woman?)

3. Marriage Customs

Although it is not stated in the story, the sheriff probably met his wife through the mail. Cowboys frequently went east to meet and marry mail-order brides. Today, Americans seldom marry someone they don't know. Why was this custom popular then? In some cultures do people still marry strangers? How are these marriages arranged? Are people happy with arranged marriages? Do they often divorce?

Role Playing

Imagine you are the sheriff with a new bride. You have just watched Scratchy Wilson walk away after he threatened to shoot you. You rush inside the house and shut the door. (In the excitement, you have forgotten to pick up and carry your new bride through the front door, as is the custom when newlyweds first enter their new home.) You are worried about how your wife feels after her rude meeting with Scratchy Wilson. She is very frightened and wonders if she will have to get used to meeting people like Wilson. Is the town full of wild cowboys who might shoot her anytime she leaves the house? Explain to your wife what happened. Assure her that she does not need to worry about gunfighters. Now imagine that you are the bride. What questions will you ask your husband? Will you demand to return to San Antonio on the next train?

Choose a partner in the class and write a dialogue as shown below. Then practice your parts until you can perform your roles in front of the class. You might begin your conversation as suggested below:

Sheriff: Well, welcome to your new home in Yellow Sky!
Bride: Who was that wild drunk out there?
Sheriff: Oh, you mean Scratchy Wilson. He's OK when he's not drinkin'.
Bride: I thought he was goin' to kill you for sure!
Sheriff: . . .
Bride: . . .

For Further Discussion: Conflict

Every good story has a *conflict,* in which two opposing forces, ideas, people, or values confront each other. Often the conflict occurs when two characters, like Wilson and Potter, fight each other. But besides the apparent conflict between the sheriff and Scratchy in the story, each character must also resolve an *inner conflict* when two values or beliefs they have do not agree. Potter was a public figure, who carried a gun and was expected to be very brave. He was also a normal man who wanted a wife. How does his desire to have a wife and family conflict with his role as sheriff? When reading the story, how do we know that he has trouble dealing with his conflicting feelings? Wilson wants to shoot the sheriff, but he also respects Potter's bride. Does Wilson feel it would be honorable to shoot an unarmed, newly married man? How does he resolve this conflict? After reading the story, how do you think cowboys felt about their wives, and about fighting and drinking? Which values were most important to them?

An Occurrence at
Owl Creek Bridge

AMBROSE BIERCE

America during the Civil War

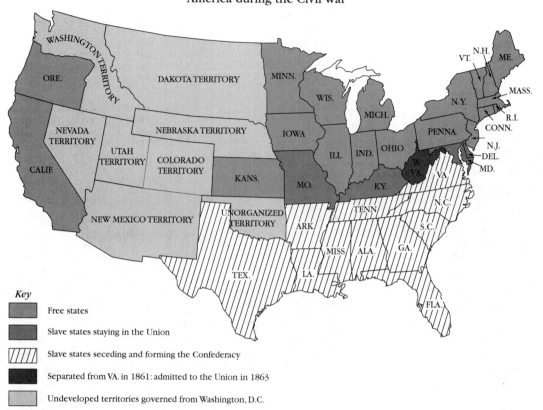

Key

- Free states
- Slave states staying in the Union
- Slave states seceding and forming the Confederacy
- Separated from VA. in 1861: admitted to the Union in 1863
- Undeveloped territories governed from Washington, D.C.

Between 1861 and 1865, the United States suffered through the Civil War, a tragic conflict that divided the nation into North (the Union) and South (the Confederacy). Causes of the war were complex, but both sides focused on the issue of slavery, the brutal institution upon which the South's agricultural economy depended.

THE AUTHOR

Ambrose Bierce, who came from a poor Ohio farming family, was eighteen when he joined the Union Army as a drummer boy. After the war he was discharged in San Francisco, a lieutenant and veteran of many battles. There he became a popular newspaper columnist and short story author. Bierce's experiences in the Civil War left him disillusioned with humanity and fascinated with death.

THE STORY

"An Occurrence at Owl Creek Bridge" is a detailed description of the execution by hanging of a Southern gentleman by the invading Union Army. This thrilling but uncomfortable story examines the power of a man's mind to deny death. Bierce reveals the great strength of man's will to live, even when faced with certain death. The story explores the question to which no living human knows the answer: Just what occurs in a person's mind at the moment that death arrives? What will we think about at the moment we die?

I

A man stood on a railroad bridge in northern Alabama, his head in a **noose**, waiting to be hanged. He looked down into the water, dark and running swiftly, twenty feet below. His hands were tied together behind his back. The rope around his neck was attached to the thick **timber** above his head, and the **slack** fell to the level of his knees. Peyton Farquhar, the condemned man, and four soldiers stood on some loose boards which had been laid across the **ties** to make a temporary platform for the **execution**. Two private soldiers commanded by a **sergeant** were inspecting the noose and the rope that tied the prisoner's hands together. Behind the sergeant on the same temporary platform, but at a distance from the man to be hanged, stood the captain. There was a guard at each end of the bridge, with rifle in hand and back turned to the scene of the hanging. Blocking the bridge was their duty. The hanging would go on without interruption.

On one side of the bridge, beyond one **sentinel**, the railroad ran straight into a forest for a hundred yards, then curved out of sight. No one could be seen. On the other bank of the bridge, on a gentle hill, a **stockade** had been built from trees cut from the forest. The barrel of a brass cannon poked through a small opening in the fortress wall. **Spectators** lined up to watch the execution—a company of infantry soldiers standing at "parade rest," the butts of their rifles on the ground, the barrels against their right shoulders. An officer, a **lieutenant**, stood to one side of the troops, holding a sword. Except for the group of four on the bridge who were preparing the man for execution, no one moved a muscle. The guards on the bridge looked like statues. Everyone was totally silent. The preparations for the hanging were being carried out

---

noose rope around the neck

timber rough board / length of rope hanging loose

slack heavy timbers supporting iron rails / formal killing / noncommissioned army officer ranking above private and corporal

sentinel guard

stockade military prison

Spectators observers at an event or show

lieutenant officer ranking below captain

The Civil War killed hundreds of thousands of Americans. Even the president, Abraham Lincoln, did not escape death. He was assassinated by John Wilkes Booth as he sat watching a play in Washington D.C., on April 14, 1865. The photo shows the hanging of four Southern sympathizers who helped plan the killing of the president.

dignified and serious

with **solemn** ceremony by the soldiers, who realized that death is always respected, even in wartime.

someone not in the military / owner of a plantation, or large farm

The man who was being hanged was about thirty-five years of age. He was a **civilian**, a gentleman, wearing the clothing of a **planter**. The prisoner, a handsome man, had a straight nose, a firm mouth, and a broad forehead from which his long, dark hair was combed straight back, falling to the collar of his well-fitted coat. He wore a mustache and a neatly trimmed beard. His eyes had a gentle, peaceful expression hardly expected from a man with a rope

having dignity; self-respecting

around his neck. This man, a **dignified** planter, was not a common criminal. But military law provides for hanging many kinds of men, including gentlemen.

After preparing the prisoner, the two privates stepped aside and each pulled away the **plank** upon which he had been standing. The sergeant turned to the captain, **saluted,** and stood, placing his feet behind the officer, who then stepped off the plank. These movements left the condemned man and the sergeant standing on the two ends of the same plank, which crossed three of the ties of the bridge. The end of the board upon which Farquhar, the condemned man, stood did not touch the fourth tie. The weight of the man to be hanged was now supported by the sergeant, his executioner. Stepping off the board would cause it to **tilt**, and the condemned man would fall between two ties.

To the man with the rope around his neck, this seemed a simple and effective method. Because his face had not been covered nor his eyes bandaged, he **observed** everything. He looked down for a moment at his feet on the board, and the water below, and then saw a piece of **driftwood** moving in the current.

He closed his eyes so that he could spend his last moments thinking of his wife and children. The water flowing beneath his feet, the fort, the soldiers, all had **distracted** him. But now he was bothered by a new distraction. Interrupting his thoughts of his loved ones was a sound he could neither **ignore** nor understand— a sharp, clear metallic banging, like the sound of a hammer ringing against steel. Slowly the sound repeated. Impatiently he waited for the next beat of the noise. The silence was **maddening**; then again he heard the loud "crash." It seemed that the time between sounds grew longer, and the noise increased in strength and sharpness with each beat. It hurt his ear like the **thrust** of a knife; he almost screamed. Then he realized: What he heard was the **ticking** of his watch.

He opened his eyes and saw the water below him. "If I could free my hands," he thought, "I might throw off the noose and jump into the stream. By diving, I could escape the bullets, and swimming hard, reach the bank, run through the woods, and get away home. My home, thank God, is still on the other side of the enemy lines; my wife and little ones are still safe from the **invaders**."

As these thoughts **flashed** through the prisoner's mind, the captain saluted the sergeant, who stepped off his end of the plank.

II

Peyton Farquhar, a wealthy planter, came from an old and highly respected Alabama family. Since he was a slave owner and active in

---

board

raised the hand to the head (traditional military sign of respect)

tip, slant

saw

wood floating in water

prevented from concentrating

pay no attention to

driving to madness

strong push, stab

rhythmic sound of watch or clock

enemies who enter territory by force / burst briefly and suddenly

politics, he was naturally an original **secessionist**, greatly devoted to the Southern cause. For reasons unnecessary to describe here, he was unable to join the brave army of the South that defended his home state against the invading Northern army. As the war dragged on, and the Northern armies approached closer and closer to his **plantation**, he waited impatiently for a chance to contribute to the war effort. The chance, he felt, would come, as it comes to all in wartime. Meanwhile he did what he could. No service was too **humble** for him to perform if it helped the South, and no adventure was too dangerous.

One evening while Farquhar and his wife were sitting on the porch of their **mansion**, a soldier dressed in the grey uniform of the South rode up and asked for a drink of water. Mrs. Farquhar was happy to serve him with her own white hands. While she went inside to get the water, her husband asked **eagerly** for news from the war zone.

"The **Yanks** are repairing the railroads," said the man, "and are getting ready to move forward again. They have reached the Owl **Creek** Bridge, about thirty miles from here. They've repaired it and built a stockade on the north bank. The Union commander has ordered that any civilian caught interfering with the railroad, its bridges, tunnels, or trains will be **summarily** hanged. I saw the order posted on countless trees and fences."

"Are there any troops on this side of the bridge?" Farquhar asked.

"Only a small **scouting patrol**, and a single sentinel at this end of the bridge."

"Suppose a man, a civilian and someone not afraid of hanging, could get by the patrol and get to the bridge, and perhaps surprise the guard on the bridge," said Farquhar, smiling, "what could he do?"

The soldier thought for a moment. "I was there a month ago," he replied. "I remember seeing that last winter's flood waters had carried a great quantity of driftwood against the wooden **pier** at this end of the bridge. That driftwood is now dry and could easily be set on fire."

Mrs. Farquhar had now brought the water, which the soldier drank. He thanked her formally, bowed to her husband, and rode away. An hour later, after dark, he passed the plantation again, but this time he rode silently, so he would not be noticed. He rode north, in the direction from which he had come. He was a Union scout in **disguise**.

men who wanted the South to leave, or secede from, the United States

large farm

lowly, unimportant

great house

with great excitement and interest

Yankees (Northerners)

body of flowing water smaller than a river

on the spot, without a trial

soldiers sent ahead of the main army to gather information

post supporting the bridge, sunk in to the creek bottom

clothing hiding a person's true identity

III

As Peyton Farquhar fell straight through the bridge, he lost **consciousness**. His mind was as if already dead. But he was awakened—ages later, it seemed to him—by a sharp pain in his throat. Then he felt the panic of **suffocation**. A sharp pain shot from his neck downward through every nerve of his body to his arms and legs.

> awareness, ability to think

> choking, inability to breathe

He felt as if he were on fire. His head was exploding from the incredible pressure. All these **sensations** he felt, but without thinking. The intellectual part of his nature was already gone. He could only feel, and feeling was only terrible, unimaginable pain. He was conscious of motion. His whole body felt like a burning ball of fire falling through a cloud. Then all at once, with terrible suddenness, the light about him disappeared with the noise of a loud **splash**. A frightful roar was in his ears, and all was cold and dark. The power of thought was **restored**; he knew that the rope had broken and he had fallen into the stream. The noose around his neck was so tight it was already suffocating him and kept the water from his lungs. To die of hanging at the bottom of a river! The idea seemed to him **ludicrous**. He opened his eyes and saw above him the light of the surface, but how distant, how **inaccessible**! He saw the light grow **fainter** and fainter as he felt his body still sinking. Then it began to brighten, and he knew that he was rising toward the surface.

> physical feelings

> sound made when something lands in water
> regained, put back

> ridiculous, very funny
> impossible to reach
> weaker, darker

"To be hanged and drowned," he thought, "that is not so bad; but I don't want to be shot. No, I will not be shot; that is not fair."

He hadn't thought about freeing his hands, but the sharp pain he felt in his wrists made him realize that they were straining to break the rope that **bound** them together. Now he gave the struggle his attention, concentrating until he could almost see the rope behind his back untie itself and fall away. Bravo! What a fine job! His arms parted and floated upward.

> tied

His own hands could be seen in front of his body in the growing light. He watched them with great interest as first one and then the other grabbed the noose at his neck. They tore it away and threw it **fiercely** aside. He saw it fall away, **wiggling** like a water snake as it sank. "Put it back! Put it back!" he wanted to shout to his hands, because the loosening of the noose had caused the greatest pain that he had yet experienced. His neck ached horribly; his brain was on fire; his heart gave a great jump, trying to force itself out at his mouth. His whole body was taken over by indescribable

> savagely, angrily /
> moving rapidly from side to side

regular movements, as of a swimmer's arms and legs / come out

high-pitched scream

sensitive, sharp

awareness through the senses (seeing, hearing, etc.) /small wave of water / touched gently, lovingly

drops of water condensed on grass and plants

in the direction in which the water was flowing

device on a gun that aids the eye in aiming

experts in shooting at marks, or targets

loudness

without pity

shots fired by many guns at the same time

stuck, caught

pain. But his hands kept moving upward, and then quickly down, in powerful **strokes,** forcing him to the surface. He felt his head **emerge**; his eyes were blinded by the sunlight; his chest expanded wildly and his lungs sucked in a great breath of air, which instantly he expelled in a loud **shriek**!

He was now in complete control of his body. All his senses were **keen** and alert. The great shock he had just experienced had sharpened his **perceptions** and made him aware of sights and sounds he had never before noticed. He felt the water against his face and heard the splash of each **ripple** as it **caressed** his cheeks. He looked at the forest on the bank of the stream, and saw each tree, its leaves and even the veins of each leaf—saw the tiny insects upon them. He noted the colors in all the **dewdrops** upon a million blades of grass. A fish slid along as he watched, and he heard the sound of its body parting the water.

He had come to the surface facing **downstream**. He turned around and saw the bridge, the fort, the soldiers on the bridge, the captain, the sergeant, the two privates, his executioners. They shouted and moved their arms, pointing at him. The captain had his pistol pointed, but did not fire. The others were unarmed.

Suddenly he heard a shot and something hit the water within a few inches of his head, splashing his face with spray. He heard a second shot and saw one of the sentinels with his rifle at his shoulder, a light blue cloud rising from the gun. The man in the water saw the eye of the man on the bridge looking at him through the **sights** of the rifle. He noticed that it was a grey eye and remembered having read that grey eyes were sharpest, and that all famous **marksmen** had them. Nevertheless, this one had missed.

The current caught Farquhar and turned him around so that he was again looking into the forest. He heard the sound of a clear, high voice that rang out behind him and came across the water with a clarity and **volume** that silenced all other sounds, even the beating of his own heart. He heard the cruel words of the lieutenant, spoken coldly and **pitilessly**, "Attention, company! . . . Shoulder arms! . . . Ready! . . . Aim! . . . Fire!"

Farquhar dived—dived as deeply as he could. The water roared in his ears, but he could still hear the explosion of the **volley** and, as he was rising again toward the surface, he swam past shining bits of metal, flattened on one end, falling slowly downward. Some of the Union bullets touched him on the face as he swam, and then fell away toward the bottom. One became **lodged** between his shirt and neck. It was uncomfortably warm and he quickly pulled it out.

As he reached the surface, **gasping** for breath, he saw that he had been under water a long time. He could see he was farther downstream—nearer to safety. The soldiers had almost finished reloading their rifles.

panting, breathing quickly

The hunted man saw all this over his shoulder. He was now swimming **furiously** with the current. His brain was working as fast as his legs and arms.

with violent energy and speed

"The officer," he **reasoned**, "will not make the same mistake a second time. It is as easy dodging a volley as a single shot. He's probably already given the command to start **firing at will**. God help me! I cannot dodge them all!"

thought logically

shooting individually as they wished

An **appalling** splash within two yards of him was followed by a loud, rushing explosion which shook the river to its **depths**! A rising sheet of water curved over him, fell down on him, blinded him, drowned him! The cannon had taken its turn. As he cleared his head, he heard the ball, **deflected** from the water's surface, cracking and smashing into the trees in the forest beyond.

terrifying, awful

bottom

bounced, turned aside

"They will not do that again," he thought. "The next time they will use **grapeshot**. I must keep my eye on the gun. To avoid getting hit, I must dive as soon as I see the smoke from the barrel. The sound arrives too late; it gets here after the cannonball. That is a good gun."

cannon shot made up of many small balls, more effective against a small, moving target

Suddenly he was **whirled** round and round—helpless in the current. The water, the banks, the forests—all were **blurred**. Caught in the **rapids**, he was pushed about so fast all he saw were streaks of color. In a few moments he was thrown upon the **gravel** at the foot of the left bank of the stream—the Southern bank—and behind a large rock that hid him from his enemies. The sudden stop and the **stinging** in his hands as they **scraped** across the gravel **reassured** him that he was still alive, and he wept with delight. He dug his fingers into the sand, threw it over himself, and thanked God he could still feel the cold, wet earth. It looked like diamonds, rubies, emeralds. He looked beyond the **pebbles** on the bank. The world was more beautiful than he had ever seen. A strange rosy light shone through the trees and the wind in their branches sounded like the music of **angelic harps**. He had no wish to escape—he was content to remain in that **enchanted** spot forever.

spun, turned

out of focus, hard to see clearly / part of a river where the current runs swiftly / small stones

sharp pain / rubbed

restored confidence

small stones

beautiful-sounding musical instruments played by angels in heaven / magical

But the roar of the cannon awoke him from his dream. The soldiers had fired him a wild farewell. He jumped to his feet, rushed up the bank, and ran into the forest.

All that day he traveled, **heading** south by the sun. The forest went on forever; nowhere did he discover a break in it, not even a dirt road. He had not known that he lived in so wild a region.

moving in a certain direction

encouraged, pushed

By nightfall he was sore, tired, and starving. The thought of his wife and children **urged** him on. At last he found a road that led him in the right direction. It was as wide and straight as a city street, yet it was empty, abandoned. No houses, no people, not even a dog could be seen. The trees, black bodies, formed a straight wall on both sides. Overhead shone great golden stars looking unfamiliar

groups of stars

and grouped in strange **constellations**. The wood on either side was full of strange noises, and once, twice, and then again he heard whispers in a strange language.

enlarged because of injury

His neck was in pain, and when he touched his hand to it, he found it horribly **swollen**. He knew that it had a circle of black where the rope had bruised it. His eyes burned; he could no longer close them. His tongue was swollen with thirst. To relieve its fever, he thrust it through his teeth into the cold air. The road seemed to

covered with a soft surface, like a carpet or rug

be **carpeted** with soft grass. He could no longer feel his feet touch the ground.

Despite his suffering, he must have fallen asleep while walking, because now he sees his own home. All is the same as he left it, all bright and beautiful in the morning sunshine. He must have traveled the entire night. As he pushes open the gate and passes up the wide white walk, he sees his wife, a fresh, cool angel, step down from the

porch

veranda to meet him. At the bottom of the steps she stands waiting, with a joyous smile, in an attitude of grace and dignity. Ah, how beautiful she is! He hurries forward with extended arms. As he is

causing loss of consciousness

about to put his arms around her, he feels a **stunning** blow upon the back of the neck; a blinding white light blazes all about him with the sound of a cannon—then all is darkness and silence!

Peyton Farquhar was dead; his body, with a broken neck, swung gently from side to side beneath the Owl Creek Bridge.

Reading Comprehension

1. Peyton Farquhar was being hanged because
   a. he killed a Union soldier.
   b. he tried to burn down the Owl Creek Bridge.
   c. he was a slave owner and a secessionist.
2. He tried to burn down the bridge because
   a. it was his duty as a Confederate soldier.
   b. he didn't want the railroad to go through his plantation.
   c. he was tricked by a Union soldier in disguise.

3. As Farquhar fell between the ties of the bridge,
    a. he immediately lost consciousness.
    b. he concentrated his thoughts on his wife and family.
    c. the rope broke.
4. Farquhar thought the officer would order the soldiers to fire at will instead of in a volley because
    a. he could avoid a volley as easily as a single shot.
    b. they had to reload their rifles.
    c. he was angry at the soldiers for missing him.
5. The condemned man told himself to watch the barrel of the cannon so
    a. he wouldn't think about the rope around his neck.
    b. he could see the smoke when the cannon was fired again, and dive to escape the cannonball.
    c. the Union soldiers wouldn't think he was a coward.
6. As he ran through the forest, escaping his executioners, he couldn't feel his feet touch the ground because
    a. the road was carpeted with soft grass.
    b. they were sore from running all day and night.
    c. he was dreaming.
7. Just as he was about to put his arms around his wife,
    a. the Union soldiers caught up with him and shot him.
    b. he realized he was dreaming.
    c. his dream ended abruptly.
8. When Farquhar was being hanged,
    a. the rope broke, but he was captured and hanged again.
    b. he imagined his escape during the last seconds of his life.
    c. the rope broke, and he escaped by swimming downstream.

Vocabulary Check

Choose the sentence below that is closest in meaning to the model.

1. The rope around his neck was attached to the thick timber above his head, and *the slack fell to the level of his knees.*
    a. His pants fell to his knees.
    b. The rope around his neck was so long that it fell to his knees.
    c. He was so afraid of dying that he could not stand up.
2. Stepping off the board would cause it to tilt.
    a. When he stepped off the board, it would tip.
    b. Walking on the board would make it tip.
    c. The plank was not level because it had been stepped on.

3. Any civilian caught interfering with the railroad will be summarily hanged.
   a. Anyone caught trying to damage the railroad will be hanged without a trial.
   b. Anyone riding the train without a ticket will be hanged next summer.
   c. Any soldier who interferes with the railroad will be hanged.
4. The friendly officer had been a Union scout in disguise.
   a. The Union soldier was disgusted by the friendly officer.
   b. The friendly officer was really the enemy wearing a different uniform to hide his true identity.
   c. The officer was friendly because he had been a Boy Scout.
5. His mind was as if already dead.
   a. Because he was dead, he was unconscious.
   b. His mind was as blank as the mind of a dead man.
   c. In his mind he was thinking about his death.
6. A sharp pain in his wrist told him that he was trying to free his hands, although he hadn't thought about it.
   a. The pain in his wrist made him realize that his hands were tied together, and he was trying to untie them.
   b. He said to himself that he had to untie his hands.
   c. He hadn't thought about his hands because his wrists hurt so badly.
7. His heart gave a great jump, trying to force itself out at his mouth.
   a. His heart pounded so strongly it felt as if it would leave his body.
   b. When he jumped off the bridge, his heart jumped into his mouth.
   c. He had a heart attack when they hanged him.
8. The great shock he had just experienced had sharpened his perceptions.
   a. Being alive after having almost died made him appreciate the beauty of life.
   b. He sharpened his knife so he could cut the rope.
   c. He was shocked that the rope had broken.

Story Summary

By answering the following questions, you will write a paragraph that summarizes the story.

Who was being hanged at Owl Creek Bridge, and why was he being executed? How would you describe Peyton Farquhar's feelings in the last moments before the sergeant stepped off the board? What happened as he was being hanged? Did he really escape? Compare what happened in fact with what the condemned man imagined in the last seconds before his death. How did Peyton Farquhar really die?

Analyzing the Text

A Story Using Flashback and Imagination

A "flashback" occurs when a story is interrupted to describe events that happened at an earlier time.

"An Occurrence at Owl Creek Bridge" is a story told in three parts.

Part 1 describes the scene in which Peyton Farquhar is hanged from the bridge by the Union Army.

When does Part 2 take place? How does this "flashback" in time help the reader understand the story?

Part 3 begins where Part 1 ends, just at that moment when the luckless Farquhar is falling from the bridge to the water below, the hangman's noose around his neck. While Part 1 takes place at the Owl Creek Bridge, and Part 2 takes place on Farquhar's plantation, where does Part 3 occur? Reread the first paragraph of Part 3, and then the last paragraph of that section. How do these two paragraphs differ from the rest of Part 3?

Interpreting Maps

Look at the map of the United States at the time of the Civil War on page 126 of this story. It shows the states that left the Union to form the Confederacy, and those states that fought against them to keep the United States together. Study the map to find the information you need to answer the following questions.

1. What new state was created as a result of the Civil War?
2. Which states practiced slavery but did not join the Confederacy?
3. How many states were there in 1861? How many states joined the Confederacy? How many remained loyal to the Union?
4. On which side of the war was the West Coast?

Grammar and Sentence Writing

The Passive Voice

A sentence whose subject receives the action of the verb is written in the passive voice.

Peyton Farquhar was executed by the Union army.

Sentences in the passive voice are formed by using the verb *to be* in the appropriate tense, followed by the past participle of the active verb.

The passive voice should be used as follows:

- To focus on the receiver of the action rather than the actor.

Peyton Farquhar was being hanged (by the Union Army).

Note in the example above it is not necessary to name the object or the person performing the action.

- To avoid naming whoever performed the action.

The glass was broken accidentally. (Instead of "John broke the glass.")

- To avoid beginning a sentence with an indefinite or meaningless subject:

My car was stolen! (Instead of "Somebody stole my car!")

- To give an order or command politely.

Cigarette smoking will not be permitted during the ceremony. (Instead of "Don't smoke during the ceremony.")

When speaking informally, Americans often substitute the verb "to get" for "to be":

They got married last week. (Instead of "They were married.")
Farquhar got caught by the soldiers. (Instead of "Farquhar was caught.")

Sentence Writing

Rewrite the following sentences in the passive voice.

MODEL:
They tied his hands together behind his back.
His hands were tied together behind his back.

MODEL:
The soldiers had laid some loose boards across the ties.
Some loose boards had been laid across the ties.

1. They couldn't see anyone.

   _____

   _____

2. They had built an army stockade from trees cut from the forest.

   _____

   _____

3. The man whom they were hanging was about thirty-five years of age.

   _____

   _____

4. He combed his long, dark hair straight back.

   _____

   _____

5. Even in wartime, everyone always respects death.

_____

_____

6. Anyone could easily set the driftwood beneath the bridge on fire.

_____

_____

7. A sharp pain in his throat awoke him ages later.

_____

_____

8. "I don't want them to shoot me."

_____

_____

9. He could see his own hands in front of his body.

_____

_____

10. The sunlight blinded his eyes.

_____

_____

11. Suddenly the current pushed and whirled him round and round.

_____

_____

12. The current threw him upon the gravel at the side of the stream.

_____

_____

13. The Union scout dressed in a Confederate uniform tricked him into trying to burn down the bridge.

_____

_____

14. It seemed as if they had carpeted the road with soft grass.

_____

_____

Appositives

An appositive is a word or phrase describing the noun it follows. It is set off from the rest of the sentence with two commas.

Example: Alabama, a slave state, was part of the Confederacy.

The executioner was a sergeant in the Union army.
He checked the rope that tied the prisoner's hands together.

The two sentences above share the same subject. They may be combined using an appositive because the first sentence is a simple predicate nominative construction. (After the verb *was,* another name for the subject is given.)

The executioner, a sergeant in the Union army, checked the rope that tied the prisoner's hands together.

Writing Appositives

Form appositives to join the following pairs of sentences so that they are written as they appear in the story.

MODEL:
Peyton Farquhar was the condemned man.
He and four soldiers stood on a temporary platform for the execution.

Peyton Farquhar, the condemned man, and four soldiers stood on a

temporary platform for the execution.

MODEL:
An officer was a lieutenant.
He stood to one side of the troops, holding a sword.

An officer, a lieutenant, stood to one side of the troops, holding a sword.

1. He was a gentleman.
   He was a civilian, wearing the clothing of a planter.

   _____

   _____

2. The prisoner was a handsome man.
   He had a straight nose, firm mouth, and a broad forehead.

   _____

   _____

3. This man was a dignified planter.
   He was not a common criminal.

   _____

   _____

4. The weight of the man to be hanged was now supported by the sergeant.
   He was his executioner.

   _____

   _____

5. Peyton Farquhar was a wealthy planter.
   He came from an old and highly respected Alabama family.

   _____

   _____

6. Suppose a man was a civilian and someone not afraid of hanging.
   Suppose he could get by the patrol and get to the bridge.

   _____

   _____

7. The trees were black bodies.
   They formed a straight wall on both sides.

   _____

   _____

8. He sees his wife.
   She is a fresh, cool angel.

   _____

   _____

   _____

Word Forms

Choose the correct word to complete each of the sentences below.

execute   executed   execution   executioners

1. Emerging from the river, Farquhar saw his _____ on the bridge
   above.

2. The Union army posted signs saying they would _____ anyone interfering with the railroad.

3. Any civilian caught interfering with the railroad will be _____.

4. The soldiers stood silently, watching the_____.

distracted   distraction   distracting

1. The soldiers were _____ Farquhar from thinking about his family.

2. The water flowing beneath his feet, the fort, the soldiers, all had _____ him.

3. Then the ticking of his watch became an even greater _____.

imagine   imagination   imagining   unimaginable

1. He could only feel, and feeling was only terrible, _____ pain.

2. Just _____ being hanged would make anyone feel uncomfortable.

3. In Farquhar's _____, the rope had broken and he was returning home.

4. Can you _____ how terrible it would be to be hanged?

uncomfortably   comfort   uncomfortable

1. In his luxurious mansion, Farquhar lived in great _____.

2. The bullet lodged between his shirt and neck was _____ warm and he quickly pulled it out.

3. Watching the execution, many of the soldiers felt _____.

Gerunds

A verb form that ends with *ing*, when used as a noun, is called a gerund.

Gerunds can be the subject of a sentence:

The *hanging* will be carried out at dawn.

Or gerunds can be the object of a sentence:

Farquhar could not remember *traveling* over this road before.

Or gerunds can be the object of a preposition:

He was looking forward to *getting* home to his wife.

Writing Gerunds

Using the suggested gerund, rewrite each sentence below as it appears in the story.

MODEL:

To block the bridge was their duty. (blocking)

Blocking the bridge was their duty.

1. The law provides for the execution of many kinds of men, including gentlemen. (hanging)

   _____

   _____

2. When he stepped off the board, he would cause it to tilt. (stepping).

   _____

   _____

3. If I dove, I could escape the bullets, and if I swam hard, I could reach the bank. (diving, swimming)

   _____

   _____

4. Suppose a man not afraid to die could get by the patrol. (hanging)

   _____

   _____

   _____

5. He could only feel, and the sensation was only terrible, unimaginable pain. (feeling)

   _____

   _____

   _____

6. When he loosened the noose it had caused the greatest pain that he had yet experienced. (loosening)

_____

_____

7. He heard a high voice that silenced all other sounds, even the sound of his own heart. (beating)

_____

_____

8. They will probably start to shoot at any second. (firing)

_____

_____

9. The sudden stop and the pain in his hands as they scraped across the gravel reassured him that he was still alive. (stinging)

_____

_____

10. Despite his pain, he must have fallen asleep while walking. (suffering)

_____

_____

Sentence Writing

Using gerunds, write sentences answering the following questions:

1. What were the sentinels responsible for doing?

_____

_____

2. What was Farquhar planning on doing when he rode to the bridge?

_____

_____

3. When he closed his eyes, what did he want to spend his last moments doing?

_____

_____

4. After he escaped the noose, what was Farquhar looking forward to
doing?

_____

_____

Developing Ideas

Guided Paragraph Writing

Was He Guilty?   1. Did Farquhar deserve to be hanged? Explain why.
He was tricked by Union soldier disguised as a Confederate. What would
have happened to the Union scout if the Southern army had caught him
wearing a Confederate uniform? Did he deserve to be hanged also? Why or
why not? Would a soldier in uniform have been hanged if he had been
captured trying to interfere with the railroad? Why or why not? Why would
a civilian have been punished more severely than a soldier?

Fantastic Dreams   2. Have you ever had a dream that seemed as
real as Farquhar's escape? No matter how fantastic it may seem, describe
what happened to you in your dream, and when you woke up and realized that what you had experienced was unreal. Describe how you felt
when you realized that you had been dreaming.

Topics for Discussion

1. The Civil War
Study the Civil War map of the United States at the beginning of this story.
Between 1861 and 1865 the Northern and Southern United States fought a
bloody civil war. Causes of the conflict were complex, but when it was
over, and General Robert E. Lee had surrendered to General U.S. Grant at
Appomattox, Virginia, all that had been proven was that no state, for what-
ever reason, could declare its independence from the United States. Was
slavery the only cause of the Civil War? Compare Civil War America with
the U.S. of today. What states joined the rebel Confederacy and what states
remained with the Union? What states did not exist at the time of the war?
What effects of this conflict can still be observed today? What does the
Confederate flag look like? When and where is it still displayed today?
What does it represent?

2. The Cynicism of Ambrose Bierce
Bierce was a cynic, distrustful of human nature and critical of social customs. He wrote of "the brave army of the North" and described the execu-

tion as a "solemn ceremony." Did he really believe that the army was brave and the execution was dignified? What do the futility of Farquhar's attempt to burn down the bridge and his imagined escape suggest about Bierce's opinion of war, death, and patriotism?

3. The Storyteller's Technique

The narration of Farquhar's escape is written in the past tense, but Bierce shifts to the present tense in the next-to-last paragraph of the story. What is the effect of this shift of tense? Does it enhance the dreamlike quality of the story? What other clues does the author leave in his writing which suggest that the escape is unreal? Look closely at Part 3, especially the last paragraphs, to find details suggesting that Farquhar is only imagining his escape.

For Further Discussion: The Surprise Ending

To hold the reader's attention, a good story usually is centered on a conflict or struggle between two forces. These forces should be closely matched in strength, so that the reader is uncertain of the outcome. When reading "An Occurrence at Owl Creek Bridge," we hope Farquhar will succeed in escaping from his executioners. However, Farquhar never had a chance. How does Bierce create suspense in a story in which the protagonist, or hero, is doomed from the beginning? At the end of the story, did you feel cheated or tricked when you found out that Farquhar had been dead all along? Why would Bierce want to trick the reader like this?

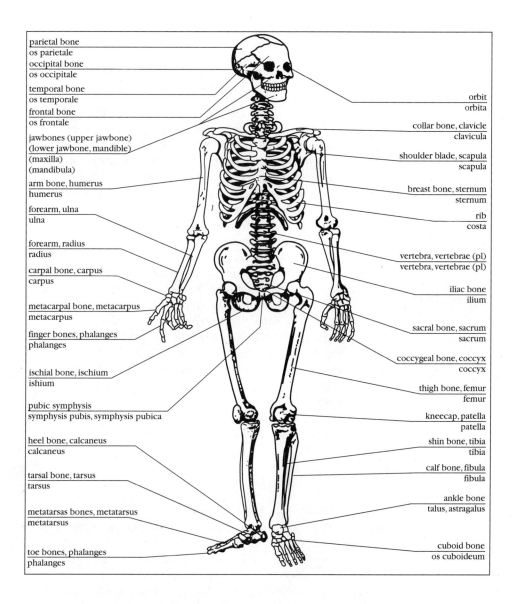

parietal bone
os parietale
occipital bone
os occipitale

temporal bone
os temporale
frontal bone
os frontale

jawbones (upper jawbone)
(lower jawbone, mandible)
(maxilla)
(mandibula)

arm bone, humerus
humerus

forearm, ulna
ulna

forearm, radius
radius

carpal bone, carpus
carpus

metacarpal bone, metacarpus
metacarpus

finger bones, phalanges
phalanges

ischial bone, ischium
ishium

pubic symphysis
symphysis pubis, symphysis pubica

heel bone, calcaneus
calcaneus

tarsal bone, tarsus
tarsus

metatarsas bones, metatarsus
metatarsus

toe bones, phalanges
phalanges

orbit
orbita

collar bone, clavicle
clavicula

shoulder blade, scapula
scapula

breast bone, sternum
sternum

rib
costa

vertebra, vertebrae (pl)
vertebra, vertebrae (pl)

iliac bone
ilium

sacral bone, sacrum
sacrum

coccygeal bone, coccyx
coccyx

thigh bone, femur
femur

kneecap, patella
patella

shin bone, tibia
tibia

calf bone, fibula
fibula

ankle bone
talus, astragalus

cuboid bone
os cuboideum

A Curious Dream

MARK TWAIN

THE AUTHOR

*Samuel Clemens grew up on the Mississippi River in Missouri
before the Civil War, when slavery was legal. After his father
died, he went to work at the age of twelve as a printer's helper.
He worked as a printer for newspapers in the East until the
age of twenty-one, when he became a boatsman on the
Mississippi River. Here he found inspiration for the pen name
"Mark Twain," in honor of those men who worked the river he
loved. But soon Twain was forced to flee West to avoid the Civil
War. He began writing, first as a newspaper reporter, and then
as a humorist.*

*In 1865 he wrote his brother from San Francisco: "I have had a
'call' to literature, of a low order—i.e., humorous. It is nothing to
be proud of, but it is my strongest suit."*

*He had started his long career as America's most popular writer,
and as an internationally famous lecturer. He wrote about the
different areas of the United States in which he lived, but his most
important writing appeared in* Huckleberry Finn, *a novel about
the adventures of two runaways—a black slave and a white
teenage boy—on a Mississippi River raft.*

*Twain lived a long life as writer, humorist, and social critic. He
died in 1910, at the age of seventy-five.*

THE STORY

*"A Curious Dream" is an example Mark Twain's ability to use
humor to call attention to human weakness. He wrote the
story for a newspaper to remind the citizens to take care of the
public cemetery, to not become so busy with their lives that
they forget about their ancestors who have died.*

*But who can speak for the Dead? Twain's dream enables the
skeletons in the cemetery to speak with a loud voice on the
editorial page of his newspaper.*

*Before reading the story, imagine what ghosts from the
cemetery would say if they really could speak from the grave.
What would they complain about? What would they want
us to do for them?*

The night before last I had the strangest dream that I have ever
had. I seemed to be sitting on a doorstep (in no particular city) half
asleep, and the time of night appeared to be about twelve or one
o'clock. The weather was warm and there was no human sound in

*Mark Twain, the well-respected author, humorist, and lec-
turer at the age of 63.*

the air, not even a footstep. There was no sound of any kind, except the occasional **barking** of a dog in the distance. Then up the street I heard a bony clack-clacking, and wondered what it was.

In a minute more a tall skeleton, **hooded**, and half dressed in a torn and **moldy shroud**, walked by me with a **stately stride** and disappeared in the gray gloom of the starlight. It had a broken and worm-eaten **coffin** on its shoulder and a **bundle** of something in its hand. I knew what the clack-clacking was then; it was this skeleton's **joints** working together, and his elbows knocking against his sides as he walked. I may say I was surprised. Before I could collect my thoughts I heard another one coming—for I recognized his clack-clack. He had two-thirds of a coffin on his shoulder, and some boards under his arm. I mightily wanted to look under his hood

> **barking** loud cry of a dog
>
> **hooded** wearing a head covering / **moldy shroud** old, rotting cloth covering the body / **stately stride** proud walk
>
> **coffin** box for burying the dead / **bundle** bunch
>
> **joints** places where bones come together

and speak to him, but when he turned and smiled at me with his empty **sockets** for eyes and his frightening grin as he went by, I thought I should not stop him. He was hardly gone when I heard the clacking again, and another one came out of the shadowy half-light. This one was bending under a heavy gravestone, and dragging a **shabby** coffin after him. When he got close he gave me a steady look for a moment or two, and then came up to me, saying:

"Help me set this down, will you? I have got to catch my breath."

I eased the gravestone down until it rested on the ground, and in doing so noticed that it belonged to "John Baxter Copmanhurst," with "May, 1839," as the date of his death. The deceased sat wearily down by me, and wiped his **os frontis** with his **major maxillary**—chiefly from former habit I judged, for I could not see that he wiped away any **perspiration**.

"It is too bad, too bad," said he, drawing his **tattered** cape about him and leaning his jaw thoughtfully on his hand. Then he put his left foot up on his knee and began scratching his ankle bone with a rusty nail which he got out of his coffin.

"What is too bad, friend?" I said, trying to be polite.

"Oh, everything, everything. I almost wish I never had died."

"You surprise me. Why do you say this? Has anything gone wrong? What is the matter?"

"Matter! Look at my robes—rags. Look at this gravestone, all **battered** up. Look at that disgraceful old coffin. It's all I've got in this world. All a man's property is going to ruin and destruction before his eyes, and you ask him if anything is wrong? It's all going to hell, if we're not there already!"

"Calm yourself, calm yourself," I said. "It is too bad—it is certainly too bad, but then I had not thought that you would care about such matters, **situated** as you are."

"Well, my dear sir, I do care. My pride is hurt, and my comfort is **impaired**—destroyed, I might say. I will state my case—I will put it to you in such a way that you can understand it, if you will let me. Please sir, you have got to listen to me," said the poor skeleton, tilting his **skull** back with confidence unusual for someone who had already been dead for years, but he was as if clearing for action, and thus demonstrating an attitude very much at **odds** with his grave position in life, or death, so to speak.

"Proceed with your story," said I.

"I **reside** in the shameful old graveyard a block or two above you here, in this street, and have for these thirty years, and I will

---

Glossary (margin):

hole in which something is put

old, worn out

Latin terms for human bones

sweat from the body

torn in pieces

hit, dented, damaged

located, placed

stopped, ruined

head bone

against, not in agreement

live, inhabit

tell you things have changed since I first laid this tired old **frame** there, turned over, got comfortable, and stretched out for a long sleep, with a delicious sense of being done with bother, and grief, and anxiety, and doubt, and fear, forever and ever, and I was listening with increasing satisfaction to the noise of the shoveled dirt on my coffin until it faded away to a faint tapping that shaped the roof of my new home under the ground.

supporting structure, bones

"Yes sir, thirty years ago I laid me down there, and was happy. It was out in the country then—out in the breezy, flowery, grand old woods, and the lazy winds blew through the leaves, and the squirrels ran over us and around us, and the crawling things visited us, and the birds filled the air with music. Oh yes, it was worth ten years of a man's life to be dead then! Everything was pleasant. I was in a good neighborhood, for all the dead people who lived near me belonged to the best families in the city. Our **posterity** appeared to think the world of us. They kept our graves in the very best condition. The fences were always repaired, statues and monuments were polished, the rosebushes and the **shrubbery** were trimmed, and the walks were cleaned and smoothed.

future generation of family members

greenery, bushes

"But that day is gone by. Our **descendants** have forgotten us. My grandson lives in a stately house built with money made by these old hands of mine, and I sleep in a **neglected** grave with invading worms that build nests within my skull! I and my friends who lie with me in there **founded** and secured the prosperity of this fine city, and now our loved ones leave us to rot in a **dilapidated** cemetery. See the difference between the old time and now. For instance: Our graves are all caved in now; our **head-boards** have rotted away and **tumbled** down. There are no roses any more, nor shrubs, nor anything that is a comfort to the eye. And now we cannot hide our poverty in the friendly woods, for the city has grown and stretched out and surrounded our graveyard. I tell you it is a terrible disgrace!

family members they produced

not taken care of

began, established

falling apart

board with name and dates of person buried underneath / fallen

"Now you begin to understand—you begin to see how it is. While our descendants are living luxuriously on our money, right around us in the city, we have to fight hard to keep skull and bones together."

A most **ghastly** expression began to develop among the **decayed** features of my guest's face, or skull, I should say, and I was beginning to grow uneasy and distressed, when he continued:

frightening, scary / rotted

"Yes, friend," said the poor skeleton, "the facts are just as I have given them to you. Two of these old graveyards—the one that I resided in and one further out—have been **deliberately** neglected

on purpose, not by accident

by our descendants of today until there is no occupying them any longer. We have got to move or see our belongings wasted away and **utterly** destroyed. Now, you will hardly believe it, but it is true, nevertheless, that there isn't a single coffin in good repair among all my **acquaintances**—now, that is an absolute fact.

"Why here come a half dozen members of the Jarvis family, carrying the family monument along. Hello, old friends. Now do you see who is walking this way? That individual going along with a piece of headboard under his arm, one leg bone below his knee gone? That is Barstow Dalhousie, the most finely dressed **corpse** to ever enter our cemetery. We are all leaving. We cannot tolerate the treatment we are receiving at the hands of our descendants. They open new cemeteries, but they leave us to our **ignominy**. They repair the streets, but they never repair anything that is about us or belongs to us. Look at that coffin of mine—yet I tell you in its day it was a piece of furniture that would have attracted attention in any living room in this city. You may have it if you want it—I can't afford to repair it. Put a new bottom in her, and part of a new top, and a bit of fresh **lining**, and you'll find her very comfortable. No, don't thank me for the gift. You have been kind to me, and I would give you all the property I have got before I would seem **ungrateful**."

"God no, please!" I **involuntarily** shouted, for somehow I was not looking for that kind of gift, and it caught me a little off my guard. But I quickly tried to make amends, saying, "I simply meant I could not accept the honor—I did not mean to speak disrespectfully of such a kind offer of yours."

"Well, just as you say, but I wish to be fair. Goodbye, friend, I must be going. I may have a good way to go tonight—I don't know. I only know one thing for certain, and that is, that I am leaving, and I'll never sleep in that crazy old cemetery again. I will travel until I find suitable quarters, no matter how far. All the boys are going. It was decided in a public meeting, last night, to **emigrate**, and by the time the sun rises there won't be a bone left in our old **habitations**.

"If you will give me a lift with this tombstone I guess I will join company with the Jarvis's. They're a mighty respectable old family. Goodbye, friend."

And with his gravestone on his shoulder he joined the **grisly** procession, dragging his damaged coffin after him, for although he offered it to me so **earnestly**, I utterly refused to take it. I suppose I sat there for about two hours watching these sad **outcasts** go by, clack-clacking, carrying their tombstones and coffins, and all that time I sat pitying them.

Margin glossary:

totally

casual friends

dead body

shame

cloth or other material covering the inside

not thankful, unappreciative / not meaning to do it

move away

homes, residences

marked by death, scary

sincerely

not wanted by society

This whole matter interested me deeply, and caused great sympathy for these homeless skeletons. And it all seeming real, and I not knowing it was a dream, I mentioned to one ghostly wanderer that an idea had entered my head to publish an account of this curious and very sorrowful **exodus** in the daily newspaper, but I was afraid that if I wrote truthfully about what I had seen it would shock and **distress** their **surviving** friends. But this ghost of a former citizen leaned his bones over my way and whispered in my ear, and said:

large group leaving together

make sad or unhappy / still living

"Do not let that disturb you. The community that can stand such graveyards as those we are leaving can stand anything you can say about the neglected and **forsaken** dead that lie in them."

abandoned, left alone

At that very moment a rooster **crowed**, and the weird procession vanished and left not a bone behind. I awoke, and found myself lying with my head out of the bed and "sagging" downwards considerably—a position favorable to dreaming strange dreams with morals in them.

loud cry of a rooster

Reading Comprehension

Circle the correct answer or answers.

1. When the narrator first met the parade of skeletons,
    a. he was visiting the cemetery.
    b. he was sitting on a doorstep in the middle of the night.
    c. he was dreaming.
2. John Baxter Copmanhurst
    a. wrote this story.
    b. died in 1839.
    c. was looking for a new cemetery.
3. The skeleton was complaining about
    a. how his old bones were clack-clacking.
    b. how the cemetery was in disrepair.
    c. how his descendants had forgotten him.
4. When the skeletons had a meeting in the cemetery, they decided to
    a. move to a better graveyard.
    b. elect a president.
    c. haunt their descendants.
5. The skeleton wanted to give the narrator his coffin because
    a. he had listened kindly while he complained about the condition of the cemetery.
    b. he knew he would soon die and would need a coffin himself.
    c. he wanted a ride to the next town.

6. The cemetery was in poor condition because
    a. the descendents of its occupants did not take care of it anymore.
    b. the people living in the town did not care about the cemetery or its inhabitants.
    c. taxes were too high, and the economy was poor.
7. People should take care of the cemeteries in their towns because
    a. the dead will haunt them if they do not.
    b. we should respect our ancestors, and their resting places.
    c. our ancestors worked hard for us when they were alive, so we should care for their graves when they are dead.
8. At the end of the story, all the skeletons disappeared because
    a. a rooster crowed as the sun began to rise.
    b. they flew away to a new town, looking for a new cemetery.
    c. the narrator woke up from his dream.

Vocabulary Check

Choose the sentence below that is closest in meaning to the model.

1. "While our descendants are living luxuriously on our money, right around us in the city, we have to fight hard to keep skull and bones together."
    a. While our grandchildren have an easy life because they inherited our wealth, we are neglected and falling apart in the cemetery.
    b. The younger members of our families who are still alive are fighting over our money.
    c. Our families have forgotten about us, their dead ancestors, and we are left to fight among ourselves in the cemetery.
2. "Look at that coffin of mine—yet I tell you in its day it was a piece of furniture that would have attracted attention in any living room in this city."
    a. My coffin was beautiful when it was new.
    b. My coffin was as beautiful as a piece of fine living room furniture when it was new.
    c. Before I was buried, everyone came to see me in my brand new coffin.
3. "God no, please!" I involuntarily shouted, for somehow I was not looking for that kind of gift, and it caught me a little off my guard.
    a. I was surprised when the guard caught me looking for that kind of gift.
    b. I did not mean to shout, but I was horrified at the thought of receiving a coffin for a gift.
    c. I shouted to God to save me from these dead spirits.
4. But I quickly tried to make amends.
    a. I quickly tried to run away from the skeleton.
    b. I quickly tried to fix his coffin.
    c. I quickly tried to apologize.

5. " I will travel until I find suitable quarters."
   a. Can you spare a quarter so I can continue traveling?
   b. I don't know how long I will be traveling.
   c. I'll continue traveling until I find a better cemetery.
6. I mentioned to one ghostly wanderer that an idea had entered my head to publish an account of this curious and very sorrowful exodus in the daily newspaper.
   a. I told one skeleton that I was thinking about writing a story in the newspaper describing the poor conditions in the cemetery.
   b. I told one skeleton that I was thinking about writing a story in the newspaper describing the strange dream I was having.
   c. I told a ghost that I thought he was just a dream that had entered my head.
7. "The community that can stand such graveyards as those we are leaving can stand anything you can say about the neglected and forsaken dead that lie in them."
   a. The people of this community should have to stand in the graveyard all night so they can see how badly they have neglected us.
   b. The people of this community do not care about their dead ancestors.
   c. Any community who treats their dead ancestors like we have been treated does not care what people say about them.
8. At that very moment a rooster crowed, and the weird procession vanished and left not a bone behind.
   a. When I heard a rooster, I woke up from my dream.
   b. When the rooster crowed, the skeletons disappeared.
   c. The skeletons disappeared at dawn.

Story Summary

"A Curious Dream" is a story told by a narrator who sees the skeletons leaving the cemetery in his dream. Now retell the story from the point of view of the remains of John Baxter Companhurst, who is leaving the place of his residence since his death in 1839.

Write two paragraphs: In the first describe what has happened to the cemetery since the skeleton died and was buried there. In the second, explain why the dead are leaving their burial grounds. Write as if you were the dead man (*"I have been buried there since . . . . I am leaving the cemetery because. . ."*).

In the same paragraph, explain the moral or lesson the skeleton's descendants should learn. Why is the skeleton unhappy with his relatives who are still alive? Pretend he is writing to his grandchildren (*You enjoy spending the money I earned when I was alive, but. . .*).

Analyzing the Text

Although the main characters in this story are skeletons and are obviously very different from living people, Mark Twain makes these old bones come alive in "A Curious Dream." The skeletons talk and act as if they were normal, living people with flesh as well as bones. Reread the story to see how many different ways Twain tricks the reader into thinking that ghosts behave like normal humans. In this way he makes the story plausible, or easier to believe.

Examples: Ghosts Who Act Like They Are Still Alive

"It is too bad, too bad," said he, <u>drawing his tattered cape about him</u> and <u>leaning his jaw thoughtfully on his hand</u>. Then he put his left foot up on his knee and <u>began scratching his ankle bone</u> with a rusty nail which he got out of his coffin.

Reread the entire story and underline the phrases like those above which describe the skeletons as if they were still alive. Note especially the way the main character describes his "life" in the cemetery.

Grammar and Sentence Writing

Using *Got* in Informal English

As Twain shows in reporting the speech of the skeleton, *"got"* is used frequently in casual American conversation. Read the following sentences which all contain *got*. It can mean "acquire" or "become," but often is a substitute for "be" or "have" in some form. In each sentence, replace the *got* phrase with other appropriate vocabulary.

1. When he <u>got close</u>, he gave me a steady look for a moment or two, and then came up to me. _____

2. I <u>have got to</u> catch my breath. _____

3. He began scratching his ankle bone with a rusty nail which he <u>got out of</u> his coffin. _____

4. It's all <u>I've got</u> in this world. _____

5. Please sir, you <u>have got to</u> listen to me. _____

6. I laid this tired old frame in my grave, turned over, <u>got comfortable</u>, and stretched out for a long sleep. _____

7. You have been kind to me, and I would give you all the property I <u>have got</u> before I would seem ungrateful. _____

8 We <u>have got to move</u> or see our belongings wasted away and utterly destroyed. _____

The Present Perfect Tense

The present perfect tense is used to describe an action that has occurred before we speak, but at an unspecified time:

> **I <u>have visited</u> that cemetery before, but I do not remember when I went there.**

The present perfect tense can also refer to an action that has happened more than once in the past, or has never happened:

> **I <u>have</u> often <u>dreamt</u> about ghosts, but I <u>have</u> never <u>dreamt</u> of talking skeletons before.**

To form the present perfect tense, use the present tense form of the verb <u>have</u> with the past participle form of the main verb:

> **The skeleton <u>has</u> not <u>eaten</u> any food since he died.**

> **For many years now, the widow <u>has gone</u> to the cemetery every spring.**

Do not confuse the present perfect tense with the simple past tense, which is used to describe a past action that occurred at a specific time:

> **She <u>went</u> to the cemetery last April. (simple past)**

Sentence Writing A

Read the following statements about "A Curious Dream," then write a sentence explaining their meaning. Use the adverbs and the present perfect tense of the verbs in parentheses to make your own sentences.

MODEL:
I would be horrified if a skeleton gave me his old, rotten coffin.
(never / give)
A skeleton has never given me his old, rotten coffin before.

The head-boards in the cemetery are all rotten.   (rot)
The head-boards in the cemetery have all rotted.

1. I would be surprised to dream about talking skeletons. (never / dream)

   _____

   _____

   _____

2. Their living relatives do not think about their dead ancestors. (forget)

   _____

   _____

   _____

3. I would be shocked to see a skeleton walking down the street.
   (never / see)

   _____

   _____

   _____

4. The skeletons do not know what they will find when they leave the
   cemetery. (never / leave)

   _____

   _____

   _____

5. Someday I would like to read *Huckleberry Finn* by Mark Twain.
   (never / read)

   _____

   _____

6. The Jarvis family are leaving the cemetery too. (decide)

   _____

   _____

7. The cemetery is their home. They were buried in 1835.
   (be *or* bury* / since)

   _____

   _____

*passive voice

Sentence Writing B

Use the simple past tense to answer the following questions about the sentences below, which each contain verbs in the present perfect tense. Use the word in parentheses to connect the time phrase with the main clause.

MODEL:
John Baxter Copmanhurst <u>has been dead</u> since May, 1839.
When did John Baxter Copmanhurst die? (in)
He <u>died</u> in May 1839.

MODEL:
The skeleton's clothes <u>have turned</u> into rags.
When did his clothes turn into rags? (after)
His clothes <u>turned</u> into rags after he died.

1. I <u>have resided</u> in that shameful old graveyard for thirty years.
   When did he move to the graveyard? (ago)

   _____

   _____

2. Things <u>have changed</u> since I first laid this tired old frame there, turned over, got comfortable, and stretched out for a long sleep.
   When did things change in the graveyard? (after)

   _____

   _____

3. Since we died, our descendants <u>have forgotten</u> us.
   When did his descendants forget him? (after)

   _____

   _____

4. Since they stopped visiting the cemetery, our head-boards <u>have rotted</u> away.
   When did their head-boards rot away? (after)

   _____

   _____

5. The city <u>has grown</u> and stretched out and surrounded our graveyard.
   When did the city surround the graveyard? (when)

   _____

   _____

6. You <u>have been</u> kind to me tonight.
   When was he kind to the skeleton? (when)

   _____

   _____

7. I would like to give you my coffin. It is all the property <u>I have got</u>.
   When did the skeleton get his "property," or his coffin? (after)

   _____

   _____

The Past and Present in the Old Cemetery

In the blanks below, write the correct form of the following verbs, using either the simple past or simple present tenses:

"Yes sir, thirty years ago I ___(lay)___ me down there, and I ___(be)___ happy. It ___(be)___ out in the country then—out in the breezy, flowery, grand old woods, and the lazy winds ___(blow)___ through the leaves, and the squirrels ___(run)___ over us and around us, and the crawling things ___(visit)___ us, and the birds ___(fill)___ the air with music. Oh yes, it ___(be)___ worth ten years of a man's life to be dead then! Everything ___(be)___ pleasant. I ___(be)___ in a good neighborhood, for all the dead people who ___(live)___ near me ___(belong)___ to the best families in the city. Our posterity ___(appear)___ to think the world of us. They ___(keep)___ our graves in the very best condition. The fences ___(be)___ always repaired, statues and monuments ___(be)___ polished, the rosebushes and the shrubbery ___(be)___ trimmed, and the walks ___(be)___ cleaned and smoothed.

"But that day ___(be)___ gone by. Our descendants ___(have)___ forgotten us. My grandson ___(live)___ in a stately house built with money made by these old hands of mine, and I ___(sleep)___ in a neglected grave with invading worms that ___(build)___ nests within my skull! I and my friends who __(lie)__ with me in there founded and secured the prosperity of this fine city, and now our loved ones _(leave)_ us to rot in a dilapidated cemetery. See the difference between the old time and now. For instance: Our graves __(be)__ all caved in now; our head-boards __(be)__ rotted away and tumbled down. There __(be)__ no roses any more, nor shrubs, nor anything that __(be)__ a comfort to the eye. And now we __(can)__ not hide our poverty in the friendly woods, for the city __(have)__ grown and stretched out and surrounded our graveyard. I tell you it __(be)__ disgraceful!

Combining Phrases and Clauses to Form a Series

Related ideas, words, phrases, or clauses can be grouped together in a series connected by commas.

Groups of words can be linked this way:

Skeletons, ghosts, and goblins inhabit old cemeteries.

Phrases can also be written in a series:

The dead spirits arose from their graves, left the cemetery, and began searching for a new home.

Independent clauses, which can stand alone as complete sentences, can also be linked in a series:

The dead are buried, their children forget about them, and their cemeteries are left to ruin.

Note that each series consists of three or more items, each separated by a comma. The last item in a series always begins with a connecting word like *and, but,* or *or.*

It was not a ghost, a talking skeleton, but only a dream.

He could tell his friends about his strange conversation, write a story for the local newspaper, or just forget about it.

Sentence Writing C

Combine the following groups of sentences into a series of phrases or clauses forming a single sentence. Use commas to separate each item in the series, and add a connecting word before the last item.

MODEL:

The skeleton owned only his old bones.
The skeleton owned the headstone from his grave.
The skeleton owned his rotten coffin.

The skeleton owned only his old bones, the headstone from his grave, and

his rotten coffin.

MODEL:

The skeleton's eye sockets were empty.
His teeth had mostly fallen out.
His cloak was a tattered rag.

The skeleton's eye sockets were empty, his teeth had mostly fallen out,

and his cloak was a tattered rag.

1. There was no moon.
   The weather was balmy.
   There was no human sound in the air, not even a footstep.

2. The skeleton's joints were working together.
   His elbows were knocking against his sides as he walked.
   I could hear the clack-clacking sound of his old bones moving against each other.

3. He eased the gravestone down to the ground.
   He sat wearily beside me.
   He wiped his os frontis with his major maxillary.

4. My pride is hurt.
   My comfort is impaired.
   My home is ruined.

   _____

   _____

5. I laid my frame to rest in my coffin.
   I turned over.
   I stretched out for a long sleep.

   _____

   _____

6. Thirty years ago the cemetery was out in the country then.
   It was in the breezy, flowery old woods.
   It was in a good neighborhood.

   _____

   _____

7. Our graves are all caved in now.
   Our head-boards have rotted away.
   Our gravestones have fallen over.
   The flowers have all died.

   _____

   _____

8. I will travel until I find respectable quarters.
   I will travel until I find a decent place to lie down my bones.
   I will travel until I find a new cemetery in which to spend eternity.

   _____

   _____

9. At that very moment a rooster crowed.
   At that very moment the weird procession vanished.
   At that very moment I awoke.

   _____

   _____

   _____

Word Forms

Choose the correct word to complete each of the sentences below.

respect   respectable   disrespect   disrespectfully

1. I guess I will join company with the Jarvis's. They're a mighty
   _____ old family.
2. Every family should _____ their ancestors.
3. "I simply meant I could not accept the honor—I did not mean to speak
   _____ of such a kind offer of yours."
4. A city that does not take care of its cemeteries shows _____
   for the dead.

shamelessly   ashamed   shame   shameful

1. I reside in the _____ old graveyard a block or two above you
   here.
2. Families who do not take good care of the graves of their ancestors
   should be_____ of themselves.
3. All the ghosts in the cemetery had to find a new place to rest their
   bones. What a _____!
4. The grandchildren of the skeleton _____ spent the money they
   inherited from him while they neglected his grave.

fright   frighten   frightening   frightened

1. As he went by, he turned and smiled at me with his empty sockets for
   eyes and his _____ grin.
2. Mark Twain was _____ by a parade of skeletons.
3. The sight of a skeleton carrying his own coffin and gravestone would
   _____ anyone.
4. When the skeleton offered to give Mark Twain his coffin, it caused him
   a great _____.

disgraceful   disgrace   disgraced

1. "Look at that _____ old coffin. All a man's property is going to ruin and destruction before his eyes."
2. "And now we cannot hide our poverty in the friendly woods, for the city has grown and stretched out and surrounded our graveyard. I tell you it is a terrible _____!"
3. The skeleton believed that his grandchildren had _____ his family name.

death   died   dead   die

1. The people under the ground in the cemetery are all _____.
2. Most people are afraid of _____.
3. But the skeletons in "A Curious Dream" had already _____.
4. Although Mark Twain was a young man when he wrote the story, he realized that someday he would _____.

Developing Ideas

Paragraph Writing

Respect for Ancestors in America   1. In many cultures families have great respect for their deceased ancestors. In fact, in some countries, ancestors play an important religious role. Compare the way Americans treat their dead family members with the way the dead are honored in other societies. Do Americans show proper respect for the dead?

Cremation: The Answer to Crowded Cemeteries?   2. When "A Curious Dream" was written in the nineteenth century, there was much more room for people in the United States, both for the living and for the dead. But as cities have grown, cemeteries have been moved to make room for new homes. The population of the country has grown, and real estate has become more valuable. *Cremation*, or the burning of a corpse and the preservation of the body's ashes, has become a popular way to deal with the dead. Little space is needed to store the remains, or they may be scattered over forests or the sea. Since the dead never abandon their resting places, sooner or later all of America would be covered with gravestones if every dead body were buried in its own separate grave. Is cremation a fitting way to honor the dead? What is the proper way to put our loved ones to rest after their deaths? Compare American burial practices with those popular in other cultures.

"A Curious Dream": A Humorous or Serious Story? 3. Mark Twain's stories have made Americans laugh for over one hundred years, but his writing has also caused them to pause and think about racial, religious, and other social problems in the United States. "A Curious Dream" is a funny story about an impossible encounter between a living newspaper man and ghosts fleeing a rundown cemetery. Was the story written to entertain readers, or did Twain have a more serious purpose? What is the message behind the story?

Topics for Discussion

1. Spirits, ghosts, and other supernatural beings:
Is it possible to communicate with the spirits of the dead? In a *séance* a spirit is contacted and speaks to living relatives through the voice of a *spiritualist*. Are they fakes? Can the dead contact us through dreams? What do different religions believe about this topic?

2. Why are we afraid of ghosts?
Do you believe in ghosts? Would you be afraid to walk through a cemetery at night? Why are so many afraid of the dark? Why would ghosts want to harm the living? What are evil spirits? Are there really devils and angels?

3. What really happens after we die?
The *afterlife* will always remain a mystery to the living. Different religions believe that the *soul*, or spirit, lives on after the body *decomposes*, or rots away. Where do we go after we die? Share different beliefs about the world of the dead with a discussion group. Class members may have very different opinions.

For Further Discussion: The Supernatural in Fiction

In the real world, only rarely do people claim to communicate with skeletons and ghosts, and they are usually not taken seriously when they do. But in the world of fiction, the supernatural is often encountered. Do readers of ghost stories believe that ghosts really exist? Why are readers so willing to suspend reality and enjoy stories like "A Curious Dream"?

Literature can be wonderful and fantastic. Reading a story by a great author like Mark Twain or Edgar Allan Poe can fill our imagination with wonders and fantasies that could never be known otherwise. Is this why so many stories about ghosts, monsters, or other fantastic characters are always popular?

- Make a list of fantastic characters, like Superman, who could never exist in real life, but who have rich lives in our imagination.
- Think about how you would feel if one day you met one of these characters. Isn't it better that superheroes and monsters exist only in the world of fiction?

The Black Cat

EDGAR ALLAN POE

THE AUTHOR

Edgar Allan Poe, the father of the mystery story, was born in 1809 to parents who were traveling actors. They both died of tuberculosis when Edgar was only two years old, and he was raised by a man named Allan, from whom Poe took his middle name. Poe attended the University of Virginia for one term, but because of bad behavior his stepfather would not allow him to return, enrolling him in the U.S. Military Academy at West Point instead. Poe hated the strict discipline of military life and so was soon expelled from West Point. With his stepmother dead, and hated by his stepfather, Poe faced the world alone. Writing was his only talent. Although he worked for various newspapers and magazines, he was always poor. In 1835 he married his fourteen-year-old cousin, and they lived in poverty until she died twelve years later. By this time the writer was a wild alcoholic who often talked of suicide. In 1849 he was found unconscious in a Baltimore street, beaten, drunk, and half-dead. He died in a hospital a few days later. His suffering inspired beautiful love poetry and many popular short stories—many about evil, insane madmen and the horrible crimes they committed.

THE STORY

"The Black Cat" is told in the first person—that is, the person telling the story is also the main character. He is in jail, waiting to be hanged for killing his wife. In the first paragraph he tells readers: "I am not crazy. . . . I am a poor victim...haunted and doomed by an evil black cat." But should the reader believe what he says? This narrator is a murderer, an alcoholic who is so miserable that he welcomes death. As you read the frightening story he reports, remember to question his judgment and perceptions. Do the policemen investigating the disappearance of his wife believe his story? Is there really such a thing as an evil black cat?

room in a prison

As I sit in this dark **cell** waiting to die tomorrow, I am writing the sad story of my life. Tomorrow I die by the hangman's noose, but before my life ends, I must tell the world the fantastic story of how I came here to this awful place. Many might think the terrible crimes I committed were the acts of an insane man, but after read-

A scene from "The Pit and the Pendulum." Horror films based on the terrifying stories of Edgar Allen Poe have thrilled generations of moviegoers throughout the world.

ing my story you will see that I am not crazy, but instead I am a poor victim, a man **haunted** and **doomed** by an evil black cat, a cat more powerful and frightening than death itself!

visited frequently by a ghost or spirit / condemned, destined to die

To understand the tragic story of my life, you must first learn of my childhood. When I was a baby everyone thought I had a sweet and gentle personality. While I was growing up, I loved animals. My parents, who loved me very much, gave me many pets to care for. Even today I can remember the happy hours I spent playing with my dog. As I grew older, my love for animals became stronger, until, as a normal young man, I fell in love and got married.

I was married early to a girl who loved animals as much as I did. While we were waiting to begin a family of our own, we filled our lives with **domestic pets**, which we loved as if they were our own children. We soon had pets of all kinds in our happy home: birds, fish, baby rabbits, two dogs, and—a cat.

animals kept in a home for companionship

This last animal was a very large and beautiful **feline** that appeared on our porch one day and was quickly **adopted** into the family. Since we found the animal, we didn't know anything of its history, but it looked like it came from a proud and fine **lineage**. It was entirely black, and very smart. The cat was very **affectionate**, and I was not a **superstitious** man, so I laughed at the popular idea that all black cats were witches in disguise.

The cat's name was Pluto, and he became my favorite pet. I alone fed the animal, which followed me everywhere around the house. Every evening, as I was reading after dinner, he would contentedly sit with me as I **petted** him. The cat was so **attached** to me that when I left the house, it was difficult to keep him from following me through the streets.

Pluto and I remained friends for several years, while my personality changed tragically. You see, I was slowly developing a weakness for alcohol, that **cursed** poison that has destroyed so many lives. The more I drank, the worse I behaved. Life became more **gloomy**, and depressing as I drank more each passing day. My wife, who faithfully loved me in spite of my weakness, became the victim of my drunkenness. I would return home drunk, yelling and **cursing** her. But not only my wife suffered as I sank into **alcoholism**. My pets, which had filled our house with love when my life was happier, now suffered from my evil **nature**. Long after I had stopped feeding and caring for them regularly, I began to **tease** and **torture** the helpless animals. But I still loved Pluto. The black cat, which had grown old as I changed from a happy young man to a sad alcoholic, continued to follow me around the house, and even slept on my bed.

But the affection I felt for old Pluto was not enough to fight off the evil effects of the liquor I had drunk when I returned home one night in an especially ugly **mood**. I called for the cat while I was taking off my coat, but he didn't immediately come to me. I felt this **rejection** was an unforgivable insult, and, when he finally appeared, I grabbed him by the neck as if to **strangle** the poor animal. I was in a drunken **rage**. While I was holding him by the neck, I took a knife from the kitchen table, and **consciously** cut one of his eyes from its **socket**! Even after many years I'm ashamed to write these words, confessing to such an **inhumane** act.

I woke up the next day with a terrible **hangover**, remembering the shameful crime I had committed against my loving cat. I was full of **guilt** and sadness, which only made me drink more to forget the memory of my evil **deed**. As time passed, the cat slowly

---

Glossary (left margin):

member of the cat family / taken in as a member of

line of descent, family

loving, tender

afraid of bad luck

stroked affectionately / bound by affection

damned, evil

dark, hopeless

swearing at / illness caused by habitual drinking / personality

amuse oneself by

annoying / cause severe pain to

state of mind

refusal to accept

kill by squeezing the neck / wild anger

deliberately, on purpose / hole in the skull for the eyeball / lacking humanity or kindness, especially toward animals / illness caused by drinking / sorrow for having done something wrong / act

recovered. He looked terrible, with one empty eye socket, but he no longer appeared to suffer any pain. He ran around the house as usual, but he was afraid to come near me.

At first I was sad that my old cat, who had followed me like a shadow for years, would no longer come to me, but then I began to **resent** him. He seemed to haunt me with that empty eye socket. He would **peek** around a chair leg, watching me, and then, when I saw him, he would quickly disappear. I knew that I had no reason to hate the cat, and that I was responsible for its **deformity**, but I was powerless to control the feeling within me. I shuddered whenever I saw Pluto. The black cat, which would **stare** at me with that empty eye, constantly reminded me of my cruelty. Finally I could take no more. One morning I placed a rope around Pluto's neck and shamelessly hung him from a tree limb in our backyard. Even as the poor suffering cat **struggled** for its last breath, I knew that I was committing a horrible sin. But my nature, which by this time was **demented** and twisted by drink, forced me to pull the noose tighter. I killed him, even as my eyes were running with tears, because I could not stand the sight of this animal, which only reminded me of how evil I had become.

The night after I had killed my cat I suffered another **tragedy**. I was awakened by the strong smell of smoke. I heard people outside, running to the house crying "Fire!" Luckily, my wife and I escaped just before the roof of our home fell in and the entire building was destroyed. As the sun was coming up the next morning, I stood **shocked**, staring at the ruins of our home which was a complete loss.

Only the brick fireplace was left standing. As I walked around the **ruins** inspecting the blackened brick chimney, I saw something that made me shudder in cold fear. There, high on the **fire-scarred** brick, was the **outline** of a cat!

No one could miss it. Neighbors remarked on this mysterious shadow. Firemen **commented** on the strange effects of flame and great heat, which they saw from time to time in their work, and assured me that the black **profile** of the cat was only a **freak of nature**. (Of course, they knew nothing of Pluto, and I didn't tell them the unhappy story of my cat.)

Having lost our home and all our possessions, my wife and I moved into a smaller house, where I continued to drink heavily to forget my bad luck and the horrible things I had done. But the frightening **impression** of Pluto on the ruined chimney stayed in my mind, and as time helped erase the fear and resentment I had

---

feel insulted by

look at from a hiding place

ugly and unnatural appearance

look steadily and directly

fought desperately

made insane

terrible event, disaster

surprised, amazed, unable to move

remains of a building after it has been destroyed / marked and blackened by flames / line that defines a shape / spoke about

side view / an unusual event with a natural cause

image, picture

felt for the cat, I began to miss my old feline companion. Late at night, while crying tears of drunken sadness, I would curse myself for the suffering I had caused Pluto. Walking home from the bars, I would often **spot stray** cats near garbage cans in some dark **alley**. I began to look for a new animal to adopt, which would take away some of my loneliness and help relieve some of the guilt I felt for killing Pluto.

One night as I sat alone in a bar, my eyes, which were half-closed from drunkenness, spotted a shadowy figure in a dimly lit corner. Looking more closely, I realized it was a black cat. Pouring some beer from my glass into a saucer, I placed it on the floor and called for the animal to come to me. The animal approached, and we quickly made friends. This cat immediately reminded me of Pluto. It was about the same size as Pluto and seemed similar in every other respect.

I asked the bartender to whom the cat belonged so that I might ask its owner if I could buy it to take home as a pet. He told me that he had never seen the cat before, that it apparently was a stray, and that he would throw it back out into the street from where it had come if I didn't take it away. That night I took the cat to my home, where it immediately became a part of the family.

Though my wife loved the new cat deeply because he reminded her of Pluto, I was the one he chose to follow around the house. My feelings for the animal were mixed, however, because on his first morning in our home, my eyes, which now were not

clouded by drink as they had been the night I picked him up, noticed something strange about the animal. He, like Pluto before him, had only one eye! My wife only felt pity for the animal because of

his **handicap**, but I began to feel a strange fear and **revulsion** upon seeing the animal. And the more I came to **despise** the cat, the more closely he would follow me about the house! I couldn't walk from one room to another without the damned cat running under my feet, almost **tripping** me. At this time I was convinced that I would go through life suffering the affections of stupid cats, which, for some reason, were especially attracted to me.

To escape the cat and my other problems, I continued to turn to alcohol. I would spend every night in some dark, cheap bar drinking until, near unconsciousness, I would stagger home to sleep

until I awoke to begin the same **routine** again the next day.

Returning home drunk one evening, I found the cat, as usual, at the door to greet me. My wife asked for some firewood from the **cellar**, so I started down the steps, when suddenly the cat ran be-

tween my legs, tripping me. I fell to the bottom, fortunately suffering only minor **bruises**. But now I was **determined** to take **revenge** on this cat. Picking up an axe that was near the pile of firewood, I swung it over my head to strike the cursed animal a **fatal**
blow. But just then, my wife, who had been attracted by the noise
in the basement, rushed down the stairs and grabbed the axe, saving the cat from death. Instantly my rage was turned against her. I
smashed the axe into her skull and she fell instantly dead, a victim
of the husband she had **faithfully** loved and served.

I stood shocked at my deed. I cried and begged God to bring
her back to life, but at least I realized that I could not undo the
wrong that I had done. The only thing I could do was to save myself from the **gallows**, so, like any common murderer, I began to
think of how to get away with this terrible crime.

I must hide the body, I knew. The street on which we lived
was busy, always filled with traffic, so I was afraid that I would be
seen if I tried to leave the house with my wife's **corpse**. I was
looking around the cellar, hoping to find a solution to my dilemma,
when I saw the building materials **stacked** in one corner.

Workmen had **piled** materials which had been left over from
construction of the house, and among the materials were some
bricks like the ones used in the **foundation**. I began to think of
ways that I could use these materials to solve my problem. A small
closet had been built into the foundation wall in which wood
could be piled. Now I had a plan!

Working quickly, I removed the wood in the **enclosure**, stack-
ing it against the opposite wall. I then placed my dead wife in the
empty space and, using some **mortar** I found with the bricks,
started to wall up the closet, so that it looked just like the rest of
the foundation wall.

It took me hours to finish the job, but finally I placed the last
brick into the wall. I went upstairs to sleep while the mortar dried.

But then I remembered the cat. That animal, who had caused
me to commit this terrible crime, must pay with his life. I looked
throughout the house for the cat, whom I planned to strangle with
my **bare hands**, but I couldn't find him anywhere. I thought he
must have been so frightened by the **bloodshed** in the basement
that he had run away, so I finally gave up looking for him.

The next morning I went into the basement to inspect my
work. The new wall I had built looked just like the rest of the
foundation. No one would ever know my wife lay buried in the
basement of her own home. Satisfied that my crime would go

discolored spots on the skin caused by injury / firmly decided / punishment inflicted in return for a wrong / death-causing

truly, steadily

wooden frame on which condemned persons are hanged

dead body

placed on top of one another / stacked, put on top of one another

the lowest part of a building, partly below ground

small, closed-off space

cement used to hold bricks together

hands only, without the use of tools or weapons / violence producing blood

undiscovered

undetected, I went to the police station to report the disappearance of my wife.

The following day, since she was still missing, the police came to the house to ask questions and search for **clues** to my wife's disappearance. I confidently welcomed them, telling a story about how she had left to do some shopping and had never returned. I assured the police that she was a faithful and loving wife, and had not run off with another man. Confident that her body would never be found, I acted like I was very worried about her.

pieces of information that help solve a mystery

After questioning me, the officers asked if they could look through the house. I said yes, of course, and then led them from room to room while they looked in closets, under beds, and through all of our drawers. Finally the detective asked me if we had a basement.

"Of course," I said. "Let me show you."

My heart was **pounding** with excitement as I thought of how close we would be standing to my wife's body.

beating hard

"We keep our wood down here," I remarked as we went down the stairs. To hide my nervousness, I talked continuously. "Notice how solid this wall is." I kicked the very same wall behind which I had hid my wife.

"Yes, gentlemen, see what a well-built house this is!" I said, as I kicked the same bricks again.

And at that moment we heard a cry from behind the wall that was so loud, so frightening, and so terrible that I welcome the **grave** that will receive me tomorrow so that I might forget its terrible sound. I **fainted**, and when I awoke the policemen had just finished opening a hole in the wall with their hammers. As they looked into the tomb with flashlights, my one-eyed black cat jumped out. It was the cry of that cursed cat that put me here in this prison, and that follows me to my grave!

burial place for a dead person / suddenly lost consciousness

Reading Comprehension

1. The narrator, or the man who tells the story, is in jail for
   a. killing his wife.
   b. killing his cat.
   c. drunk driving.
2. When he was a child, he
   a. was often violent.
   b. loved animals.
   c. thought cats were evil.

3. He cut out his cat's eye because
   a. the cat followed him too closely.
   b. it didn't come when he called it one night.
   c. he hated all cats.
4. The narrator claims that his violent nature is caused by
   a. alcoholism.
   b. cats.
   c. poverty.
5. Very soon after he killed his cat,
   a. he started drinking.
   b. his wife died.
   c. his house burned down.
6. All that remained of this house after the fire was
   a. some cat food.
   b. the chimney with the cat's image burned on it.
   c. the basement where he buried his wife.
7. The narrator killed her because
   a. she tried to defend the black cat.
   b. she had another lover.
   c. she burned his dinner.
8. The police found his wife's body because
   a. he confessed to the crime.
   b. the cat, which had hidden in the tomb, cried out when the police
      were in the basement.
   c. a neighbor had seen the burial and informed the police.

Vocabulary Check

Choose the sentence below that is closest in meaning to the model.

1. I was not a superstitious man, so I laughed at the popular idea that all
   black cats were witches in disguise.
   a. I had a good sense of humor, so I laughed at the cute behavior of
      my black cat.
   b. I didn't believe that black cats were really evil witches.
   c. Because I didn't believe in any religion, I was not afraid of black
      cats.
2. I was slowly developing a weakness for alcohol, that cursed poison that
   has destroyed so many lives.
   a. I wanted to drink more and more liquor, the drug that has ruined
      so many lives.
   b. I became so weak from drinking that I ruined my health.
   c. One night when I was drunk I tried to destroy my life by drinking
      poison.

3. My nature by this time was demented and twisted by drink.
   a. I enjoyed the beauties of nature when I was drunk.
   b. Alcohol had changed me into a terrible person.
   c. Drinking gave me a more pleasant personality.
4. There, high on the fire-scarred brick, was the outline of a cat!
   a. My cat was standing on the chimney.
   b. My cat was buried behind the bricks.
   c. The fire had left a smoke stain in the shape of a cat.
5. The black profile of the cat was only a freak of nature.
   a. The outline of the cat on the chimney was merely a mark left by the fire.
   b. The cat was a freak because it had only one eye.
   c. Black cats are nature's most beautiful animals.
6. The impression of Pluto on the ruined chimney stayed in my mind.
   a. Pluto was so impressed with me that he always stayed in my presence.
   b. I couldn't forget the picture of Pluto that we saw on the chimney after the fire.
   c. When Pluto wandered onto our porch, he made a good impression on me.
7. Now I was determined to take revenge on this cat.
   a. I really wanted to pay back the cat for the trouble he had caused me.
   b. I am in jail because the cat is paying me back for the terrible things I did to it.
   c. I found out that the cat came from a good background.
8. We heard a cry from behind the wall that was so loud, so frightening, and so terrible that I welcome the grave that will receive me tomorrow so that I might forget its terrible sound.
   a. The cat cried so loudly that even the dead in their graves could hear it.
   b. I'll be glad when I am dead so that I can share my grave with the black cat.
   c. I was so frightened by the cry of the black cat that I'll be glad when I am dead and can no longer remember its terrible sound.

Story Summary

By answering the following questions, you will write a paragraph that summarizes the story.

Who tells the story, and where is he telling it from? What has he done to be put in this place? What caused him to do it? Why did he adopt the black cat into his family? Did he believe that the cat might be evil?

Why? What caused him to cut out the cat's eye? Why did he kill the cat? What bad luck did he then suffer? Why did he want another black cat? How did this cat get revenge?

Analyzing the Text

Although the story is titled "The Black Cat" the narrator believes there have been <u>two</u> black cats in his life. He writes that he killed Pluto, the first black cat, in a drunken rage.

The second cat, which he found in a bar one night, revealed to the police the location of the narrator's dead wife. Remember, this was also the same cat who made his owner so mad that he murdered his wife in a blind rage.

Were there two cats, or only one? Was the second cat a reincarnation of Pluto, taking revenge for his cruel death? After all, some say cats have nine lives. Reread those paragraphs of the story in which the narrator first meets the second cat, takes him home, and then notices that he, like Pluto, has only one eye. What other sentences in the story suggest that these two cats might be the same? Where did this new cat come from?

Grammar and Sentence Writing

Relative Clauses: *Who* and *Which*

My parents loved me very much.
They gave me many pets to care for.

Related ideas like those above can be joined together by using *relative pronouns:*

My parents, who loved me very much, gave me many pets to care for.

Use the relative pronoun *who* when the subject is a person. Use *which* (or *that*) for other subjects referring to animals or things:

We filled our lives with pets.
We loved them as if they were our own children.

Because both of the above sentences refer to the same object (*pets*), they can be joined together by using *which:*

We filled our lives with pets, which we loved as if they were our own children.

Sentence Combining

Combine the following sentences as shown in the models below.

MODEL:

My parents loved me very much. They gave me many pets to care for. (who)

My parents, who loved me very much, gave me many pets to care for.

MODEL:

We filled our lives with domestic pets. We loved them as if they were our own children. (which)

We filled our lives with domestic pets, which we loved as if they were our

own children.

1. I was married early to a girl. She loved animals as much as I did. (who)

2. This last animal was a very large and beautiful feline. He appeared on our porch one day. (which)

3. I alone fed the animal. He followed me everywhere around the house. (which)

4. My wife faithfully loved me in spite of my weakness. She became the victim of my drunkenness. (who)

5. My pets had filled our house with love when my life was happier. Now they suffered from my evil nature. (which)

6. The black cat had grown old as I changed from a happy young man to a sad alcoholic. He continued to follow me around the house. (which)

   _____

   _____

7. My old cat followed me like a shadow for years. Now he would no longer come to me. (which)

   _____

   _____

8. The black cat would stare at me with that empty eye. He constantly reminded me of my cruelty. (which)

   _____

   _____

9. My nature by this time was demented and twisted by drink. It forced me to pull the noose tighter. (which)

   _____

   _____

10. I could not stand the sight of the animal. He only reminded me of how evil I had become. (which)

    _____

    _____

11. I began to look for a new animal to adopt. It would take away some of my loneliness. (which)

    _____

    _____

12. My eyes were half-closed from drunkenness. They spotted a shadowy figure in a dimly lit corner. (which)

    _____

    _____

13. My eyes were not clouded by drink as they had been the night I picked him up. They noticed something strange about the animal. (which)

    _____

    _____

14. I would go through life suffering the affections of stupid cats. They, for some reason, were especially attracted to me. (which)

_____

_____

_____

15. My wife had been attracted by the noise in the basement. She rushed down the stairs and grabbed the axe. (who)

_____

_____

_____

Using Commas to Set Off Relative Clauses

Edgar Allan Poe, who wrote "The Black Cat," lived a tragic life.
The man who wrote "The Black Cat" lived a tragic life.

Both of these sentences contain the same relative clause—*who wrote "The Black Cat"*—but the first clause is set off with commas, and the second is not. This is because in the first sentence the clause is not needed to understand who the antecedent is. (Every relative clause has an antecedent, which is the noun in front of the *who* or *which*.) When the relative gives added information, but is not essential, it is set off with commas.

However, when the relative clause is needed to understand the sentence, it is not set off with commas.

Any man who kills his wife should be hanged.

If we left out the relative clause *who kills his wife,* the sentence would read:

Any man should be hanged.

Because the meaning of the sentence would be changed without it, the relative clause is essential and does not need commas to separate it from the rest of the sentence.

The narrator of the story, who killed his wife, should be hanged.

In the above sentence the relative clause can be omitted without changing the meaning:

The narrator of the story should be hanged.

Don't use commas if you can leave out the relative clause and still identify the antecedent. Use commas to set off clauses when they can be omitted from the sentence without changing its meaning.

Commas in Relative Clauses

Place commas as needed in the following sentences.

1. Peter Allan who raised the young orphan never adopted Poe.

2. However, he was married to a woman how loved Edgar as her own son.

3. But Allan's wife died, and he married a woman who had children of her own.

4. After he remarried, Poe's stepfather who disliked the boy's wild behavior forgot all about the young writer.

5. Any man who suffered as much as Poe should be pitied.

Sentence Completion A

Using the following relative clauses, write your own complete sentences. The clauses in these sentences do not need to be set off with commas.

MODEL:
The cat that the narrator found in the bar ...

The cat that the narrator found in the bar only

had one eye.

1. The girl who became his wife . . .

_____

2. The man who wrote "The Black Cat" . . .

_____

3. The outline of the cat that was burned onto the chimney . . .

_____

4. The police who came to his house . . .

_____

5. . . . a disease that is caused by excessive drinking.

_____

Sentence Completion B

Complete the following sentences with your own words. These relative clauses are nonessential, so they need commas.

MODEL:
Poe, who wrote "The Black Cat," . . .
Poe, who wrote "The Black Cat," died of alcoholism.

1. He hated the one-eyed cat, which . . .

2. The narrator of the story, who . . ., wrote the story in jail.

3. In a drunken rage the narrator killed his wife, who . . .

4. After removing the bricks, the police found his wife's body, which . . .

5. He was the victim of an evil black cat, which . . .

Sentence Writing

Write two sentences using each relative clause below. One sentence should use a nonessential *who* or *which* clause (it will need commas); the second sentence should have an essential relative clause (without commas).

MODEL:
who kills a black cat

(a) The narrator, who kills a black cat, has very bad luck.

(b) Anyone who kills a black cat will have bad luck.

1. who had only one eye

(a)

(b)

2. who has been a faithful wife for many years

(a) _____

_____

(b) _____

_____

3. who is waiting in prison to die

(a) _____

_____

(b) _____

_____

4. who he found in a bar one night

(a) _____

_____

(b) _____

_____

***When to Use So and* Very**   *So* as a modifier is used only in complex sentences that describe a causal relationship. Always use *very* in simple sentences.

> **The narrator was very drunk.**
> **He was so drunk that he killed his wife.**

Sentence Combining

As shown in the models below, combine the following pairs of sentences using *so, so that,* or *so much that.*

MODEL:
We loved animals very much. We treated them as if they were our own children.

We loved our animals so much that we treated them as if they were our

own children.

MODEL:
The cat was very beautiful and proud. We thought it had come from a fine background.

The cat was so beautiful and proud that we thought it had come from a

fine background.

1. The cat was very attached to me. When I left the house, it followed me through the streets.

   _____

   _____

2. I drank too much. My life became gloomy and depressing.

   _____

   _____

3. I was full of guilt and sadness. I drank even more to forget the memory of my evil deed.

   _____

   _____

4. I hated that cat. I knew I had to kill him. (so much)

   _____

   _____

5. The black outline of the cat was very clear. Even the neighbors remarked on this mysterious shadow.

   _____

   _____

6. I missed him very much. I wanted another cat to take his place.

   _____

   _____

7. I was very drunk. I didn't notice that this cat also was missing an eye.

   _____

   _____

8. He followed me very closely. He tripped me and I fell down the stairs.

   _____

   _____

9. I was very angry. I was determined to have revenge on this cat.

   _____

   _____

   _____

10. I was very shocked. I cried and begged God to bring her back to life.

_____

_____

11. The street where we lived was very busy. I was afraid I would be seen if I tried to leave the house with the body.

_____

_____

12. He was very frightened by the bloodshed in the basement. He ran away.

_____

_____

Sentence Completion C

Using the clauses below, add your own words to form complete sentences. Write the _entire sentence_ in the space provided.

1. Poe's life was so unhappy that . . .

_____

_____

2. The narrator of "The Black Cat" drank so much that . . .

_____

_____

3. His wife loved him so much that . . .

_____

_____

4. He was so angry at the cat for tripping him that . . .

_____

_____

5. The scream of the cat frightened him so much that . . .

_____

_____

6. As a young boy he loved animals so much that . . .

_____

_____

Word Forms

Choose the correct word to complete the sentences below.

superstition superstitious superstitiously

1. Many people believe the _____ about black cats.

2. They _____ believe that they have evil powers.

3. But the narrator of "The Black Cat" was not _____.

alcohol alcoholic alcoholism

1. When Poe died, he was an _____.

2. He spent every evening in bars drinking _____.

3. He was a victim of the common illness called _____.

unconscious unconsciousness consciously

1. One night, while drunk, the narrator _____ cut out his cat's eye.

2. He would drink until he fell _____.

3. When he awoke from _____, the police were making a hole in the wall.

affection affectionate affectionately

1. As I read in the evenings, my cat sat on my lap, _____ purring.

2. My wife and I felt great _____ for all our pets.

3. The black cat was a very _____ animal.

shame ashamed shameful

1. Torturing animals is _____ behavior.

2. The narrator was _____ of his drinking.

3. The one-eyed cat reminded him of his _____.

Developing Ideas

Paragraph Writing

Is Luck Real?   1. Write a paragraph describing someone you know who is superstitious. Does this person think he or she has bad luck? What are some things that he or she believes cause bad luck or good luck? Give an example of something that happened to this person that he or she thought was caused by bad luck. Why do you think people often blame their problems on bad luck?

Do Pets Make Good Friends?   2. The narrator of the story has many pets. Have you ever had a close animal friend? If you have a pet that you love, write a paragraph describing it. You may write about a pet you have now or one you enjoyed as a child. Tell what it looks like, how it behaves, and why you love this animal. If you don't have a pet, or can't write about a pet you used to love, write about the kind of animal you would like to have. Would you want a pet like the Black Cat, which would follow you around the house? Or would you prefer a less affectionate pet, like a goldfish, which would stay in its tank? Describe the kind of pet that you could love, just as the narrator of "The Black Cat" loved his Pluto.

Edgar Allan Poe   3. Why do you think Poe wrote such an unhappy story? Was his life so sad that he couldn't imagine a story with a happy ending? Or did his heavy drinking twist his mind so much that horror stories seemed natural to him? Poe lived a short, unhappy life, but he is remembered by millions around the world. Was his suffering worth the fame he found after death? Do you feel sorry for him? Why? How could he have lived a happier life? Would he still be famous today if his life had been different?

Topics for Discussion

Form a small group with some of your classmates and discuss the following topics:

1. Superstitions
The dictionary defines *superstition* as a "belief resulting from ignorance." Many people believe that some animals, actions, or even numbers and days of the week can bring good or bad luck. Why are superstitions so popular? In the United States, the number seven is linked with good luck, while thirteen is considered an unlucky number. Are different numbers in

other countries considered lucky or unlucky? Compare popular superstitions in other countries with American beliefs. Are there good reasons for believing in superstitions?

2. Pets

Many visitors are impressed with the great love Americans have for their pets. Large sections of supermarkets contain pet food, pet toys, and even clothing for animals. Are animals treated the same way in other countries? Why are Americans so generous toward their domestic animals? Do you think it is wasteful to give so much to pets when there are humans who need food? If Americans were closer to their families, would they still love their pets as they do now? What do pets give their owners in return for care and love?

3. Horror Stories

Many of Poe's stories, like "The Black Cat," feature violence, bloodshed, and madness. These stories have been popular for over a century, and have been made into successful films. Horror stories and movies are one of the more popular forms of entertainment. Why do people enjoy such stories? Did you enjoy reading "The Black Cat"? Discuss some other horror stories or films that you are familiar with. What do these stories have in common? Do they usually have surprise endings? Do they make the reader afraid? Can anything be learned from reading horror stories or watching terrifying movies, or are they simply harmless entertainment? Should children be allowed to read stories like "The Black Cat"? Why or why not?

For Further Discussion: The Narrator

Who tells the story of "The Black Cat"? How is the narrator involved in the events of the story? How does this differ from the way the other stories in this book are told? Because "The Black Cat" is the tragic story of the narrator's own life, does he tell it differently than an uninvolved third person might tell it? Is his description of the cat objective? Do you believe, as the narrator says, that the cat is evil? When the story is told in the first person, by the main character, why should the reader always question and interpret what the narrator says? What are some of the reasons that the storyteller of "The Black Cat" may have misunderstood some of the terrible events of his life? If the story were told by an outsider, would it be as interesting? How would the beginning have to be changed? Why is it effective when the narrator uses his own words to describe how he feels when he injures and then kills his cat, murders his wife, tries to hide her body, and is finally caught when the cat cries out from her tomb? (Before answering, carefully reread these parts of the story.)

Rip Van Winkle

WASHINGTON IRVING

THE AUTHOR

Washington Irving was born in New York City in 1783, just two years after the end of the Revolutionary War, when the American colonies won their independence from Great Britain. Irving's father, who fought for independence alongside General George Washington, named his son after the commander-in-chief of the colonial army. Irving is sometimes called "the father of American literature" because he was one of the first to write about the people of North America. Like many American authors and artists of his time, Irving spent much of his life in Europe, where he found a large audience interested in his stories of New York and its people.

THE STORY

When reading "Rip Van Winkle," we can see early in the story that Rip, the main character, has a conflict with his wife and that the problem of his marital relationship is the main conflict that must be resolved. Something will have to happen to stop the fighting between the husband and wife before the story can end. But how does a marriage with such serious problems usually end up? Today, divorce is common, but in the time of Rip Van Winkle there must have been other ways for husbands and wives to live peacefully after their marriage had gone bad. But Rip escapes his nagging wife in a surprising way that few readers would guess!
Before reading the story, think of the many ways a husband and wife might solve the problem of an unhappy marriage. Think of modern solutions, but also consider what was commonly done in older times and in other cultures where divorce is not an easy option.

New York City was first called New Amsterdam because it was **founded** by the Dutch, the first Europeans to **claim** that part of North America. Before there were any other means of transportation, the great river that met the Atlantic Ocean at New Amsterdam was the only way into the huge **wilderness** that is now the state of New York. This river was called the Hudson, after the Dutch sea captain and explorer, Henry Hudson.

As Henry Hudson and his crew sailed up the mighty river for the first time, they must have wondered at the beauty of the

set up, established / assert ownership of

wasteland

The story takes place in a small village in the state of New York both before and after the American Revolution. After New York became part of the independent United States of America, this new flag would have flown over the village square. Note the thirteen stars representing the original thirteen states of the Union.

Catskill Mountains, whose peaks rise high to the west, **dominating** the surrounding country. Every change of season, every change of weather, and even every hour of the day change the colors and shapes of these mountains.

    The Dutch settlers followed Hudson up the valley, building small villages of little brick houses like those they had left behind in Holland, learned to use the mountains to **predict** the weather. Before a storm would come to the valley, the color of the peaks would change to a dark and **threatening** shade.

    After the English won control of the colony and named it New York, the Catskills continued to cast their changing shadows on the villages below, where the children of the men and women who came from Holland continued to live peaceful, unchanging lives.

towering over

tell in advance

menacing, indicating harm or evil

The United States of America in 1800

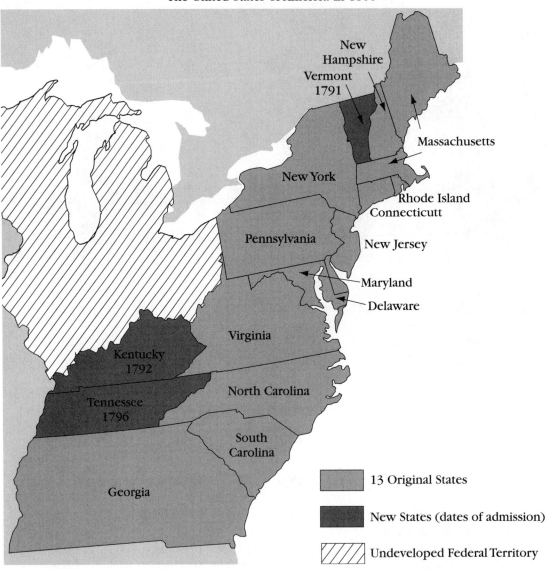

Map showing the original thirteen states of the United States of America, plus three states added before 1800.

In one of these villages, in a small old house built by his father before the King of England claimed his land, lived Rip Van Winkle.

Van Winkle, whose **ancestors** had been early Dutch settlers, lived with his wife, two children, and his dog on a small farm. He was a simple, good-natured man, a kind neighbor, and an obedient, **henpecked** husband.

lineage, previous family

(informal) dominated by his wife

The villagers liked Rip because he was always ready to help with their **chores** and burdens. It seemed that Rip Van Winkle was always happy to take care of anybody's business but his own. He would never refuse to help a neighbor do even the roughest work, before he had fed his own cows or had **tended** his own garden. The village women, whose own husbands were too busy to lend a hand, employed Rip to do their **errands** and odd jobs. They felt sorry for this helpful, kindhearted man, whose own wife never stopped **nagging** him about the work he neglected on his farm.

> daily jobs around the house
>
> taken care of
>
> short trip for a specific purpose
>
> annoying by constantly complaining

Even the children of the village were happy to see Rip approach. He played with them in their games, made them rough toys, taught them to fly kites and shoot marbles, and told them long stories of ghosts, witches, and Indians.

But Rip Van Winkle, whose farm was the most **barren** piece of property in the country, never had time to do his own chores. He found it impossible to work on his own farm or take care of his own children. It wasn't that Rip was lazy; he was always busy doing one odd job or another. It was just that Rip Van Winkle was totally **opposed** to any kind of **profitable labor**.

> unproductive, not fruitful
>
> against / money-making work

Before Rip could begin to do some important outdoor work, it seemed, it would always start to rain. Before he could fix the fence that was falling down, a neighbor would ask Rip to help him shoe a horse, and his own animals would run away. **Weeds** grew quicker in his fields than any other crop, and his **livestock** was always losing weight. After years of **neglect**, the farm he had **inherited** from his father had become more and more worthless, and his wife had become more and more unhappy with her husband.

> worthless wild grasses or plants / farm animals
> lack of care / received as a legacy

His children, too, were as **ragged** and wild as if they belonged to nobody. His son Rip, who looked just like him, inherited the habits, along with the old clothes, of his father. He was usually seen running at his mother's heels, wearing a pair of his father's old pants, which he had to hold up with one hand because they were so big.

> tattered, dressed in rags

Rip Van Winkle was one of those happy people who take life easy, eat white bread or brown, whichever is cheaper, and would rather **starve** on a penny than work for a **pound**. If left to himself, he would have whistled life away in perfect contentment, but his wife kept yelling in his ears about his **idleness**, his carelessness, and the ruin he was bringing the family. Before her husband could find a comfortable chair in which to sit, morning, noon, and night, her tongue was always going. Rip had only one way of **replying** to all his wife's lectures. He shrugged his shoulders, shook his head,

> suffer from lack of food / unit of money used in England and its colonies
> laziness, refusal to work
>
> answering

rolled

cast up his eyes, but said nothing. This, however, only made his wife more angry, so finally he would have to leave the house.

Rip's only friend at home was his dog Wolf, who was just as henpecked as his master. Dame Van Winkle considered the dog to be Rip's companion in idleness, and she never had a kind word for the animal. When out in the woods, Wolf was as brave as any other dog, but when he heard the **shrill** voice of Dame Van Winkle, his tail curled between his legs in fear and he sneaked about the house.

painfully high-pitched

Times grew worse for Rip Van Winkle as years of marriage passed. A bad temper never **mellows** with age, and after Van Winkle's wife had practiced nagging for years, she became even more effective for driving poor, **miserable** Rip from his home each day.

softens, tones down

very unhappy

Usually after Dame Van Winkle had chased Rip and Wolf from the house, the two would walk to the village square, where they met the other idle men of the town. All the men of the village who didn't have any work to do would **gather** on a bench in front of the George the Third Inn, whose name honored the ruling **monarch** of England. There they would spend a long, lazy day, talking over village **gossip**, or telling endless, sleepy stories about nothing.

come together

king or queen

idle talk or rumors, especially about the private lives of other people

Sometimes, after a traveler left an old newspaper behind, conversation became more serious. Derrick Van Bummel, the schoolmaster, and Nicholas Vedder, the oldest settler in the village and the **landlord** of the inn, would join in discussing the most important stories in the **outdated** paper. The village men, whose ideas about politics were simple and of little importance to the government that ruled them from London, nevertheless enjoyed arguing about the great political questions of the day.

owner of land and the property on it / replaced by something newer

But soon Dame Van Winkle began following Rip to the village square, where she would **scold** her husband and his friends for their idleness. Even Nicholas Vedder, whose position in the village was one of great respect, was not **immune** to her **verbal** attacks. She angrily charged the proud old man with encouraging her husband in habits of idleness.

angrily or harshly criticize

protected from / in words

Now the only place Rip could go to escape was the woods of the Catskill Mountains, so he became accustomed to **wandering** off, gun in hand, to **hike** up into the hills with his dog.

roaming, traveling around without a goal / walk a long distance

It was on a typically sunny autumn afternoon, after Rip had been chasing **fowl** high up the slopes, when he found himself in one of the highest parts of the Catskills. Rip sat down on a rock to enjoy the view. Through the trees he could see all the lower coun-

wild game birds

try for many miles. At a distance he saw the Hudson River, far, far below. On the other side he saw a deep mountain valley, whose rough floor was filled with **boulders** fallen from the surrounding **cliffs**. Then he said to his dog, whose tail wagged in friendship, "Poor Wolf! **Thy** mistress leads thee a dog's life, but never mind, my boy, as long as I live **thou** shalt never need a friend to stand by **thee**!" His dog looked up with such a **pitiful** face that Rip felt he must understand his poor master's unhappiness. He sat there for some time enjoying the view before he realized that it was getting late. It would be dark before he got home. With a heavy sigh, Rip thought of the loud welcome he would receive from his wife.

huge rocks

steep walls or slopes

your (archaic; used in seventeenth century) / you (archaic subject pronoun) / you (archaic object pronoun) / asking for pity

Before he could stand up to leave, he heard a strange voice in the distance, **hollering** "Rip Van Winkle! Rip Van Winkle!" His dog Wolf barked and then ran to his master's side, growling at something in the valley below them. Looking down, Rip saw a strange man slowly climbing up the rocks, struggling with a heavy load on his back.

(informal) yelling loudly

Rip was surprised to see another human in such a lonely part of the mountains, but because the man knew his name, he thought he must be someone from the village. So, as was his habit, he ran down into the **canyon** to help a neighbor with a heavy load.

mountain valley with very steep sides

But after Rip had climbed down into the canyon closer to the stranger, he was surprised at the man's appearance. The short, **stout** old gentleman, whose clothing was of the old-fashioned Dutch style, had **bushy** hair and a rough beard. He carried on his shoulder a heavy **keg** that seemed full of liquor, and **gestured** for Rip to come down and help him with his load. Although Rip was a little shy and somewhat distrustful of his new **acquaintance**, he climbed down. The funny-looking man seemed to know where he was going, so Rip struggled along behind, helping lift the load up the hill. As they neared the top of the slope, he heard a distant **rumble** that he thought must be thunder.

bulky, overweight

like a bush / barrel

signaled with the hand; motioned

person recently met

low, heavy sound

Once at the top, they started down a narrow **path**, and Rip heard another loud rumble, which seemed to come from a **clearing** at the end of the path. During this time the two men labored in silence. Because the man seemed so strange, and seemed so sure of where he was going, Rip was afraid to ask him any questions.

walkway in the woods

open place without trees

After they entered the clearing, Rip was even more surprised. Hearing the loud noise again, he looked up to see a group of odd-looking people playing a game of **ninepins**. Rip was amazed at their clothing. They wore short jackets with long knives in their belts and had enormous trousers, similar to the pants his strange

bowling game played with a ball and pins

person who helps
another find the way /
strange, unusual

leader of troops

from Flanders, a
region in Holland /
living room of a
home / minister,
preacher / dedicated
to, concentrated on

signaled with the hand;
gestured

ninepin players

sank to a lower level

liquid for drinking

small taste of a liquid

evil

wooden or metal end
of a gun to which the
barrel is attached

small, bushy-tailed
rodent

guide wore. Even their physical characteristics were **peculiar**. One had a large head, broad face, and tiny eyes; another had a huge nose and wore a white hat with a big red feather. They all had beards of different shapes and colors. There was one who seemed to be the **commander**. He was a stout old gentleman, with a weather-beaten face, who wore a broad belt, high-crowned hat and feather, red stockings, and high-heeled shoes with roses in them. The whole group reminded Rip of the men in an old **Flemish** painting hanging in the **parlor** of Dominic Van Shaick, the village **parson**, which had been brought from Holland with the first Dutch settlers.

These men with the strange clothing and faces, whose attention was **devoted** to their game, hardly seemed to notice Rip and the little man with the keg. Rip's companion began emptying the keg into large cups and passed the liquor to the men. He **motioned** for Rip to help him. Rip was so frightened that he obediently began to help serve the strange group of **bowlers**, whose cups emptied quickly as they drank without speaking.

Little by little Rip's fear **subsided**. After watching the others drink, he decided, when no one was looking, to taste the **beverage** himself. He took a **sip** and was surprised to taste an excellent beer, tasting much the same as imported Holland ale. He was naturally a thirsty fellow, and was soon tempted to drink another cup. One taste led to another, and he returned to the keg so often that soon, before he realized it, he had fallen into a deep sleep.

After he woke up, he found himself on the mountain knoll where he had first seen the strange little man. Rubbing his eyes, he realized that it was a bright, sunny morning. Birds were hopping among the bushes, and an eagle flew overhead in the cool morning air. "Surely," thought Rip, "I have not slept here all night!" He remembered what happened before he fell asleep—the strange man with the keg climbing up the rocks, the rumble of the ninepins, the strange bowlers, and the powerful brew. "Oh, that strange beer! That **wicked** liquor!" thought Rip. "What excuse shall I tell Dame Van Winkle?"

He looked around for his gun, but instead of his clean, well-oiled rifle, he found an old rusty gun whose **stock** had been half eaten by worms. He now suspected that the little men of the mountain had tricked him, drugging him with their strange liquor and then robbing him of his rifle. Wolf, too, had disappeared, but he might have just run off after a **squirrel** or bird. He whistled and shouted, but Wolf did not come, nor did he bark. The only sound Rip Van Winkle heard was the echo of his own cries.

Finally, he decided to go back to the scene of the ninepins game and, if he met any of the party, to demand his dog and gun. After rising to walk, he was surprised to find himself terribly stiff in the **joints**. "These mountain beds are not good for my health. And if this little adventure should give me **rheumatism**, I shall have a terrible time with Dame Van Winkle," he said to himself as he stretched his stiff arms and legs.

movable parts where two bones join, such as knees and elbows / disease that makes moving arms, fingers, and legs painful

He descended the mountain until he came to the clearing that had been the scene of the game of ninepins, but he found no one. Rip, whose growling stomach reminded him that it had been a long time since he had eaten, did not know what to do. He wanted to find the men who had stolen his gun and his dog, and he surely did not want to face his wife, but neither did he want to starve in the mountains. Looking around the clearing, he could see nothing to suggest that a party had taken place on this spot the night before. A **puzzled** Rip shook his head, and, carrying the rusty old gun he had found when he awoke, he began the long walk towards home.

confused, uncertain

As he neared the village he met a number of people, but no one he knew, which surprised him because he thought he knew everyone who lived in this **isolated** country. Their dress, too, was of a different fashion. But the people Rip Van Winkle passed stared at him just as **curiously** as he stared at them. They all pointed at his chin and grinned broadly. Rip felt his chin in curiosity, and to his **astonishment** he found that his beard had grown to be over a foot long!

cut off from the outside world

with great interest

amazement, surprise

When he came to the outskirts of the village, a gang of strange children began to follow him, laughing and pointing at his long grey beard. The dogs, too, none of which he recognized, barked at him as he passed. Even the village itself had changed. It was larger, and there were many more people in its streets. There were rows of houses that he had never seen before, and those which he remembered had disappeared. Strange names were over the doors— strange faces at the windows—everything was strange. He didn't trust his own memory. Surely this was his village, which he had left only the day before. There were the Catskill Mountains. There was the Hudson, whose waters ran as smoothly and silently as ever. But the town looked very different. Rip was greatly confused. "That keg last night," he thought, "mixed up my poor head sadly."

With some difficulty he found his own house, which he approached cautiously, expecting every moment to hear the shrill voice of Dame Van Winkle. But he found the house in ruins. The roof had fallen in, the windows had been broken, and the doors had fallen off their **hinges**. He entered the house, which had always been spotlessly clean, but found only dust and **cobwebs**. He called loudly for his wife and children, and after no one answered, Rip began to cry sadly, grieving for his lost family.

At last he ran from the **abandoned** house. He could find out what had happened to his family in the village square, at the George the Third Inn.

But when he arrived at the square he saw that it, too, had changed. In the center there stood a tall flagpole with a red, white, and blue flag that Rip had never seen before. The inn was still there, but a large sign in front **proclaimed** it the "General George Washington."

There was, as usual, a crowd in front of the inn, but Rip recognized no one. His appearance, with long beard, rough clothing, and rusty old gun, quickly attracted the attention of the crowd. With great curiosity men began asking him "on which side he planned to vote" and if he was "a Federal or a Democrat." Rip, who didn't understand what they were talking about, couldn't answer. Then a man wearing a cocked hat, stepped up to him and asked, "What brings you to the election with a gun? Do you mean to start a riot in the village?"

Rip quickly answered, "I am a poor quiet man, a native of the place, and a loyal subject of the King, God bless him!"

Immediately the crowd began to shout. "A **Tory**! A Tory! A spy! A refugee! Take him away! Lock him up!" Rip assured the crowd as best he could that he meant no harm, but had only come to the inn looking for some old friends.

"Well, who are they? Name them!" he was commanded.

Rip thought for a moment and asked, "Where is Nicholas Vedder?"

There was a short silence. Then an old man replied, "Nicholas Vedder is dead and gone for eighteen years! There was a wooden **tombstone** in the churchyard that told when he died, but that's **rotten** and gone, too."

"Where's Van Bummel, the schoolmaster?" a confused Rip asked.

"He went off to war. Some say he was killed at Yorktown, but no one's sure. He never came back."

Rip's heart felt sad at finding himself so alone in the world, his friends dead, his family disappeared. He cried out in **despair**, "Does anybody here know Rip Van Winkle?"

"Oh, Rip Van Winkle!" answered two or three. "Certainly! There he is over there, leaning against that tree!"

---

devices that allow doors to swing open and shut / spider webs

deserted, not lived in by anyone

formally announced, identified as

American colonists loyal to the British during the Revolutionary War

marker above a grave
decayed, fallen to pieces

hopelessness

Rip looked and saw a **precise** copy of himself as he looked before he awoke from his strange sleep on the mountain. Now he was totally confused. Just as he realized he didn't know who he was any longer, the man in the cocked hat demanded, "Who are you, stranger?"

"God knows!" said Rip. "I'm not myself—I'm somebody else. That's me over there. I was myself last night, before I went to sleep, but when I woke up this morning in the mountains they'd changed my gun, and everything's changed now, and I'm changed and I can't tell what's my name or who I am!"

The people now began to **nod** at one another, **tapping** their fingers against their foreheads. Some whispered that they should take the gun away from the old man, before he hurt someone.

Just then a pretty young woman pushed forward to see what was attracting all the attention. The baby she was carrying began to cry when he saw Rip.

"Hush, Rip," she said. "Hush, you little fool. The old man won't hurt you."

In some way the woman seemed familiar to Rip.

"What is your name, my good woman?" he asked.

"Judith Gardenier."

"And your father's name?"

"Ah, poor man, Rip Van Winkle was his name, but it has been twenty years since he left home with his gun and his dog, and he never has been heard of since. His dog came home without him, but whether he shot himself or was carried away by the Indians, nobody can tell. I was just a little girl then."

Rip had another question, but he was almost afraid to ask it.

"Where's your mother?"

"Oh, she, too, died a short time after. She got so angry at a traveling salesman who tried to cheat her that she burst a blood vessel and had a stroke. She dropped dead on the spot."

Rip felt at least a little comfort in this last news. The man could control himself no longer. "I am your father!" he cried. "Young Rip Van Winkle then—old Rip Van Winkle now! Does anybody know poor Rip Van Winkle?"

Everyone stood amazed, until an old woman came forward and, **straining** to look closely at old Rip, exclaimed, "Sure enough! It is Rip Van Winkle—it is himself! Welcome home again, old neighbor. Why, where have you been these twenty long years?"

Rip told his story quickly enough, because the whole twenty years had been spent as one night. Some of the neighbors believed

---

exact, identical

shake the head up and down to show understanding / lightly hitting

making a great effort

him, but most just shook their heads, until Peter Vanderdonk, whose opinion was respected by all, spoke up. The old man remembered Van Winkle at once, and told everyone that the Catskill Mountains had always been haunted and that his father told him that the great Henry Hudson returned every twenty years, with the crew of his ship, the *Half Moon*. His father himself had once seen them in old Dutch clothing playing at ninepins in a mountain valley, and many of the old settlers had heard, on a summer afternoon, the sound of their bowling, like distant thunder.

Soon the crowd broke up and returned to the election. Rip's daughter took him home to live with her. She had a good house and an ambitious young farmer for a husband, whom Rip remembered as one of the village children who used to climb on his back. Rip's son, whose personality was the same as his father's, was employed to work on the farm, but he never got anything done.

Rip now resumed his old habits. He found some of his old friends, and made many new ones from the younger generation. Since he had nothing to do at home and had no wife to restrict him, he took his place once more in front of the inn. Rip enjoyed his old age, an age when, at last, a man can be idle with **impunity**.

protection from punishment

Reading Comprehension

1. Rip Van Winkle
   a. came from Holland but lived in New York.
   b. lived in Holland.
   c. was born and lived in a village in New York founded by his Dutch ancestors.
2. Rip's wife always nagged her husband because
   a. he drank too much.
   b. he neglected his own family and farm.
   c. she had a headache.
3. Rip's farm was barren because
   a. he never did his own chores, so nothing grew there but weeds.
   b. he had inherited it from his father.
   c. it was not profitable.
4. The other people in the village
   a. disliked Rip because he was so lazy.
   b. felt sorry for him because his wife never stopped nagging him.
   c. all spoke the Dutch language.

5. Rip Van Winkle hiked up into the Catskills to
    a. go fishing and take a nap.
    b. go hunting and escape his wife.
    c. go bowling and drink beer.
6. Rip helped the little man carry the keg up the mountain because
    a. he was thirsty and wanted to drink.
    b. he was invited to the game of ninepins.
    c. it was his habit to lend a hand whenever asked.
7. The strange men playing ninepins were
    a. the ghosts of Henry Hudson and his crew of Dutch sailors.
    b. Tories, or settlers that remained loyal to England during the Revolution.
    c. just a dream Rip Van Winkle had when he fell asleep.
8. Although he had slept for twenty years of his life, Van Winkle was happy at the end of the story because
    a. he had found his dog and rifle.
    b. as an old man, he could spend his time as he wished.
    c. the United States had own its independence.

Vocabulary Check

Choose the sentence below that is closest in meaning to the model.

1. Rip Van Winkle was an obedient, henpecked husband.
    a. Rip Van Winkle took care of the chickens.
    b. Rip Van Winkle obeyed the hens.
    c. Rip Van Winkle was dominated by his wife.
2. Rip would rather starve on a penny than work for a pound.
    a. Rip would rather go hungry than work for a good meal.
    b. Rip was starving because he only had a penny.
    c. Rip would lose a pound if he stopped eating.
3. Rip was totally opposed to any kind of profitable labor.
    a. Rip would never do any work to help himself or his family.
    b. Rip hated all workers.
    c. Rip objected to sharing profits with the laborers.
4. Even Nicholas Vedder was not immune to Dame Van Winkle's verbal attacks.
    a. Dame Van Winkle injured Nicholas Vedder when she attacked him.
    b. Dame Van Winkle had a stroke when Nicholas Vedder tried to cheat her.
    c. Dame Van Winkle yelled at all the men, even Nicholas Vedder.
5. Rip hiked high up the slopes chasing fowl.
    a. Rip chased the man with the keg high up in the mountains.
    b. Rip fell when he was chasing birds in the mountains.
    c. Rip walked high up the mountainsides hunting birds.

6. After rising to walk, he was surprised to find himself terribly stiff in the joints.
    a. After he woke up, he didn't know where he was.
    b. After he stood up, he found his rifle.
    c. When he tried to walk, his arms and legs hurt when he moved them.
7. Rip enjoyed his old age, an age when, at last, a man can be idle with impunity.
    a. Rip was happy as an old man because he didn't have to work and could do whatever he wished.
    b. Rip was a happy old man because he lived with his daughter.
    c. Rip was a happy old man because he wasn't punished for sleeping for twenty years.

Story Summary

By answering the following questions, you will write a paragraph that summarizes the story.

Who was Rip Van Winkle and where did he live? Why did he climb up into the Catskill Mountains? Whom did he meet there? What was he carrying? Describe what happened when Rip followed the stranger with the keg. When he woke up, what did Rip think had happened to him? Why was Rip confused when he returned to his village? How did he find out that he had been asleep for twenty years? What happened to Dame Van Winkle? How did Rip spend his old age?

Analyze the Text

"Rip Van Winkle" takes place during the time when New York changed from a British Colony to one of the original thirteen states of the United States of America. Washington Irving describes changes in the name of the local inn and in the flag flying in the village square to highlight this important political event. After waking from his long sleep, Rip was surprised that the people of his village were angry when he told them he was "a loyal subject of the King." He did not realize that he had slept through the Revolutionary War and he was now a citizen of the United States.

But the reader also learns of events that occurred before the time of Rip Van Winkle, when Dutch explorers led by Henry Hudson were the first Europeans to visit the area, then called New Amsterdam.

Reread the story to find references to the early Dutch explorers. How do we learn of the early history of the Catskills and the

Hudson River Valley? Look carefully at the description of the strange men Rip meets in the mountains. How are they dressed? What are they drinking? Who were they? Reread the ending of the tale for the answer to this mystery.

Interpreting Maps

Look at the map of the United States on page 192 of this story. It shows the states that originally formed the United States, and those new states that were formed before 1800.

Study this map and the one included in the introduction to Chapter 4 to find the information you need to answer the following questions.

1. Compare Massachusetts today with the original state. What new state was formed within its boundaries?
2. What other states have changed their shape and size?
3. Compare Virginia on this map with the modern U.S. map. How has the state changed? To discover what caused these political changes, refer to the map in Chapter 6, which shows the United States during the Civil War.

Grammar and Sentence Writing

Joining Sentences with *Whose*

Rip Van Winkle's ancestors came from Holland.
He lived in a small village in New York.

The relative pronoun *whose* can be used to join two related sentences like those above.

Rip Van Winkle, whose ancestors came from Holland, lived in a small village in New York.

The relative clause beginning with *whose* can be placed after the subject and set off with commas, as in the sentence above, or it can be placed after the object at the end of the sentence:

He was married to Dame Van Winkle.
Her temper was very short.

He was married to Dame Van Winkle, whose temper was very short.

Reread the story of Rip Van Winkle, looking for sentences with relative clauses beginning with *whose*.

Sentence Combining

MODEL:

They must have wondered at the beauty of the Catskill Mountains. Their peaks dominated the surrounding country.

They must have wondered at the beauty of the Catskill Mountains, whose

peaks dominated the surrounding country.

MODEL:

Rip Van Winkle's ancestors had been early Dutch settlers. He lived with his wife and children on a small farm.

Rip Van Winkle, whose ancestors had been early Dutch settlers, lived with

his wife and children on a small farm.

1. The village women's own husbands were too busy to lend a hand. They employed Rip to do their errands and odd jobs.

   _____

   _____

2. They felt sorry for this helpful, kindhearted man. His own wife never stopped nagging him about the work he neglected on his farm.

   _____

   _____

3. Rip's farm was the most barren piece of property in the country. He never had time to do his own chores.

   _____

   _____

4. The men would gather in front of the George the Third Inn. Its name honored the ruling monarch of England.

   _____

   _____

5. The village men's ideas about politics were simple and of little importance. Nevertheless they enjoyed arguing about the great political questions of the day.

   _____

   _____

   _____

6. Nicholas Vedder's position in the village was one of great respect. He was not immune to Dame Van Winkle's verbal attacks.

_____

_____

7. He saw a deep mountain valley. Its rough floor was filled with boulders fallen from the surrounding cliffs.

_____

_____

8. Rip spoke kindly to his dog.
Its tail wagged in friendship.

_____

_____

9. The short, stout old gentleman's clothing was of the old-fashioned Dutch style.
He had bushy hair and a rough beard.

_____

_____

10. The men's attention was devoted to their game.
They hardly seemed to notice Rip and the little man with the keg.

_____

_____

_____

11. Rip's growling stomach reminded him that it had been a long time since he had eaten.
He did not know what to do.

_____

_____

_____

12. There was the Hudson.
Its waters ran as smoothly and silently as ever.

_____

_____

_____

Joining Sentences with *Before* or *After*

Before the English won control of New York, it was called New Amsterdam.
After the English claimed the colony, they changed its name to New York.

To show the time relationship between two related sentences, use *before* or *after* to combine them. The relative clause beginning with *before* or *after* can be placed at the beginning of the sentence, as in the examples above, or it can follow the main clause:

Rip Van Winkle had been a henpecked husband before he awoke from his long nap in the Catskills.
New Amsterdam was called New York after it became a British colony.

When both clauses share the same subject, the dependent clause can be shortened to a gerund phrase. (See p. 142)

Before awakening from his long nap, Rip Van Winkle had been a henpecked husband.
The British called the colony New York after winning it from the Dutch.

In the following exercise, use *before* or *after* to join the sentences as shown in the sentences above.

Sentence Combining

MODEL:
A storm would come to the valley.
The color of the peaks would change to a dark and threatening shade.
(before)

Before a storm would come to the valley, the color of the peaks would

change to a dark and threatening shade.

MODEL:
The English won control of the colony and named it New York.
The families of the original Dutch settlers continued to live peaceful lives.
(after)

After the English won control of the colony and named it New York, the

families of the original Dutch settlers continued to live peaceful lives.

1. Rip could begin to do some important outdoor work.
   It always started to rain. (before)

   _____

   _____

2. Rip could fix the fence that was falling down.
   A neighbor would ask him to help him shoe a horse. (before)

   _____

   _____

3. His wife had practiced nagging for years.
   She became even more effective in driving poor, miserable Rip from
   his home each day. (after)

   _____

   _____

4. A traveler left an old newspaper behind. Conversation became more
   serious. (after)

   _____

   _____

5. He stood up to leave.
   He heard a strange voice in the distance. (before)

   _____

   _____

6. Rip had climbed down into the canyon.
   He was surprised at the man's appearance. (after)

   _____

   _____

7. They entered the clearing.
   Rip was even more surprised. (after)

   _____

   _____

8. He watched the others drink.
   He decided to taste the beverage himself. (after)

   _____

   _____

9. He woke up.
   Twenty years had passed. (before)

   _____

   _____

10. They should take the gun away from the old man.
    He hurt someone. (before)

    _____

    _____

11. Rip enjoyed his old age.
    His wife had died. (after)

    _____

    _____

Archaic Language

Language is always changing. At the time of Rip Van Winkle, in the eighteenth century, the English language was different than it is today. A familiar second-person form was used that has since been abandoned. While this form is no longer used, it is important to be able to recognize it because it often appears in old but still widely read works of literature. When speaking to his dog in the story, Rip uses this familiar second person form:

> **thou = you (subject pronoun)**
>
> **thee = you (object pronoun)**
>
> **thy = your (possessive adjective)**
>
> **thine = yours (possessive noun)**

The difference between _thou_ and _thee_ is similar to the difference between _I_ and _me. Thou_ is used for the subject of a sentence:

> **Thou art a good dog.**

Thee is used as an object, after a verb or preposition.

> **I will always take care of thee.**

Two other archaic forms, _shall_ and _shalt_ (will), appear in the story.

Rewriting Archaic Language

Rewrite the following passages, changing the archaic words to modern English.

1. "Poor Wolf! Thy mistress leads thee a dog's life, but never mind, my boy, as long as I live thou shalt never need a friend to stand by thee!"

_____

_____

_____

_____

_____

_____

_____

2. "What excuse shall I tell Dame Van Winkle?"

_____

_____

_____

_____

_____

_____

_____

Word Forms

Choose the correct word to complete each of the sentences below.

nagging (adjective)   **nagging** (participial; see p. 62)
nagging (gerund; see p. 142)   **nag**

1. Dame Van Winkle was always _____ Rip about his laziness.

2. Each day Rip Van Winkle was driven out of his own home by his wife's

   _____ .

3. Poor Rip's _____ wife made his life miserable.

4. Whenever he tried to relax, she would _____ him so harshly

   that he would have to leave the house.

idle   idleness   idly

1. Rip's wife nagged him about his _____.

2. The _____ men of the village would spend the day gossiping in front of the inn.

3. Rip spent his days hiking _____ with Wolf through the Catskills.

curious   curiously   curiosity

1. Rip's _____ led him to taste the stranger's beer.

2. The _____ village children followed the old man with the long white beard.

3. The strangers stared at Rip just as _____ as he stared at them.

astonish   astonished   astonishment

1. To his _____, he found that his beard had grown over a foot long.

2. Rip was _____ to find his beard had grown to be over a foot long.

3. It would _____ anyone to wake up after sleeping for twenty years.

Developing Ideas

Paragraph Writing

Before and After: A New Nation Is Born   1. Begin your paragraph by writing: "My name is Rip Van Winkle, and I've seen a lot of changes in my life." Then compare and contrast Rip's world *before* and *after* he took his long nap. Use sentences with "Before I fell asleep, . . ." and "After I awoke, . . ." Discuss the change in government, the size of the village, his ruined house, the name of the inn, and other changes in Van Winkle's life.

An Unhappy Marriage   2. Rip and Dame Van Winkle did not have a very happy marriage. What could they have done to improve their relationship? Write a paragraph to Rip and another to Dame Van Winkle in which you suggest things they could do and say to each other to make their life together happier.

Topics for Discussion

Form a small group with some of your classmates and discuss the following topics.

1. Domestic Relations

The way family members, especially husband and wife, get along with one another is called *domestic relations*. As is seen in "Rip Van Winkle," an unhappy relationship made a man so miserable that he preferred to sleep his life away. Should Rip and his wife have tried to communicate with each other instead of constantly fighting? What would a modern-day Rip do if he had a wife who drove him out of the house daily? What would Dame Van Winkle do today if she had a husband who didn't support her family? Of course, divorce was uncommon in Colonial America. Are people more fortunate today because spouses who can't get along with each other can get divorced?

2. Historical Background

Irving's story takes place during an exciting period in American history, when the nation was first born, a child of the British Empire. Rip tells the village people that he is "a loyal subject of the King," hoping to convince them that he is friendly. But the villagers are insulted and want to put him in jail. Why? What has changed since Rip fell asleep? Is it his fault he still thinks the British king is his rightful ruler? Why was the name of the inn changed? What was the strange flag that Rip saw in the village square?

3. Sleeping for Twenty Years

Discuss what you would do if you awoke after a twenty-year nap. What would you want to do first? Would you look for your family? Try to catch up on sports or soap operas? Check your financial investments? See what changes had happened in world politics? Would you owe twenty years of back taxes? Would you try to resume your old life, or change your name and begin a new life? Would anyone believe your story?

Role Playing

What would have happened if Rip had faced his marriage problems and gone with Dame Van Winkle to visit a marriage counselor? What if they openly discussed their problems with a helpful third person? Form a group of three students: Rip, Dame Van Winkle, and the marriage counselor. Write a script and rehearse your skit before presenting it to the class.

For Further Discussion: The Curious Theme of "Rip Van Winkle"

After reading a story like "Rip Van Winkle," you might naturally ask what significance, message, or theme can be deduced from such a strange tale. Was Washington Irving trying to suggest that sleeping away one's life is preferable to facing one's problems? If Irving simply wanted to entertain his readers with a humorous tale, why is this funny story so sad? Dame Van Winkle, who died in a fit of temper over a trivial matter, and Rip Van Winkle, who slept his life away, have such exaggerated faults that no reader would identify with them, but don't we all suffer to a lesser degree the problems of the Van Winkles? Can a serious theme be found in "Rip Van Winkle," or does the story simply make us laugh because it exposes human faults and weaknesses?

Credits

Page 1, Historical, Immigrants to the U.S., Topham/ The Image Works, **Page 3**, The Statue of Liberty, Library of Congress/ Corbis, **Page 29**, Jack London, *South of The Slot,* Henry E. Huntington Library and Art Gallery, **Page 31**, Market Street area of San Francisco in the 1930's, Culver Pictures, **Page 54**, O.Henry, *The Gift of the Magi,* Philadelphia Museum of Art, given by Mrs. Cyrus McCormick, **Page 55**, "Adoration of the Magi" 1961, Bernard Buffet, © ARS, NY/Art Resource, **Page 74**, Well tended gravestones, Eastcott/Momatiuk/The Image Works, **Page 76**, Portrait of New England style woman, Jackson Archives/ The Image Works, **Page 98**, Stephen Crane, *The Bride Comes to Yellow Sky,* From the Collection of David R. Phillips, **Page 100**, Cowboy working cattle, Horace Bristol/Corbis, **Page 125**, Ambrose Bierce, *An Occurrence at Owl Creek Bridge,* Military Order of the Loyal Legion and the U.S. Army Military History Institute, Carlisle Barracks, PA, **Page 128**, Co-conspirators of John Wilkes Booth being hanged in the jail yard, July 7, 1865, Corbis, **Page 149**, Sam Clemens, The Image Works Archives, **Page 167**, Edgar Allan Poe, *The Black Cat,* Library of Congress, **Page 169**, Movie still from "The Pit & the Pendulum", The Kobal Collection, **Page 189**, Washington Irving, *Rip Van Winkle,* National Gallery of Art, Andrew Mellon Collection, **Page 191**, American flag with 13 stars, Joe Sohm/The Image Works